Careers in Focus

FILM

SECOND EDITION

Ferguson's

An Infobase Learning Company

Careers in Focus: Film, Second Edition

Copyright © 2012 by Infobase Learning

Ferguson's
An imprint of Infobase Learning
132 West 31st Street
New York NY 10001

Library of Congress Cataloging-in-Publication Data

Careers in focus. Film. — 2nd ed.
    p. cm.
    Includes bibliographical references and index.
    ISBN-13: 978-0-8160-8041-0 (hardcover : alk. paper)
    ISBN-10: 0-8160-8041-0 (hardcover : alk. paper)   1. Motion pictures—
Vocational guidance.   I. J.G. Ferguson Publishing Company.   II. Title: Film.
    PN1995.9.P75C37 2011
    791.43023—dc23

                                                              2011018837

Ferguson's books are available at special discounts when purchased in bulk quantities for businesses, associations, institutions, or sales promotions. Please call our Special Sales Department in New York at (212) 967-8800 or (800) 322-8755.

You can find Ferguson's on the World Wide Web at
http://www.infobaselearning.com

Text design by David Strelecky
Composition by Newgen North America
Cover printed by Yurchak Printing, Landisville, Pa.
Book printed and bound by Yurchak Printing, Landisville, Pa.
Date printed: October 2011
Printed in the United States of America

10 9 8 7 6 5 4 3 2 1

This book is printed on acid-free paper.

Table of Contents

Introduction

The film industry holds a place in the American imagination like no other, while also maintaining a firm hold on the American pocketbook. The U.S. movie-going public spends more than $10 billion annually at the box office. We head to movie theaters to see the latest action blockbusters and "chick-flicks." We rent and purchase our favorite films on DVD or watch them online or on our smartphones, iPads, or via other technology. We subscribe to many cable channels devoted to the 24-hour repeats of recent and classic productions. We read magazines and books about filmmaking and visit Web pages devoted to our favorite stars and movies. Some of us follow our favorite stars through Twitter. And thousands of people go beyond just being fans and decide to head to Hollywood every year with a dream of becoming an actor, screenwriter, or director.

Careers in Focus: Film describes a variety of careers in this glamorous, yet highly competitive, industry—on movie sets that range from Hollywood soundstages, to the windswept deserts of Tunisia, to the bustling city streets of Tokyo; in animation, production, and recording studios; in business offices; and in countless other settings. There are film careers for creative people who like to be the center of attention (actors and stunt performers); people who are creative, but like to work behind the scenes (production designers, costume designers, cinematographers, composers and arrangers, screenwriters, and special and visual effects technicians); people with business acumen (producers and talent agents and scouts); and people who enjoy the more technical aspects of the industry (audio recording engineers and lighting technicians).

Although formal education is available for most careers in the film industry, creativity, talent, ambition, perseverance, and "knowing the right people" are often the true keys to making or breaking a career in this highly competitive industry.

Salaries can range from nearly nonexistent for struggling actors to millions of dollars for well-known directors, producers, actors, and others in the industry. The average weekly earnings for movie industry workers were $627 in 2008 (or $32,604), according to the U.S. Department of Labor (DOL). This amount is slightly higher than the weekly average for workers in all industries.

The DOL predicts that employment in the motion picture and video industries will grow faster than the average for all industries through 2018. The growth of the cable television industries, the increasing number of viewing options for movie lovers (theaters, Internet, mobile telecommunications devices, etc.), and the growing interest in American cinema in foreign countries should create good opportunities for film professionals.

Several trends will continue to shape the move industry. Experts predict that big budget films will likely maintain their rule of the industry. Production companies will hire the most popular big-name actors and directors to draw huge profits. There has also been a renaissance in animation as a result of advances in computer technology. Some of the most popular movies of recent years have been animated films such as *Shrek, WALL-E,* and *Up.* Another major animation trend is the emergence of high-quality animation in a variety of genres that is geared toward adults. Two examples of animated features in this trend include *Persepolis* and *Waltz with Bashir,* which were nominated for Academy Awards in 2007 and 2008, respectively. Visual effects are being used increasingly on all films; filmmakers use computers to create crowd scenes, detailed backdrops, and other elements common in films. In fact, the quality of computer-generated characters and scenery is so good in some movies that audiences have not been able to tell the difference between live action and computer-generated elements. Approximately 60 percent of the scenes in the movie *Avatar,* which won the Academy Award for visual effects in 2009, were computer generated.

Today, movie production is inseparable from the TV industry. Companies make films to be released in theaters, but also plan for future rentals and downloads, as well as sales and TV showings. Feature films are more frequently produced specifically for release on TV, on both network and cable, and then released on DVD.

Change is constant in the film industry. New technology, for example, is constantly emerging that improves production techniques, as well as the viewing experience of the public. Movie genres rise and fall in popularity. The "it" actor of today may be an afterthought tomorrow. Movies are no longer just viewed in theaters or on televisions, but now on computers, MP3 players, video game consoles, and other handheld electronic devices such as the iPad. One thing is certain: People will continue to watch movies and there will continue to be exciting career opportunities for those with drive, ambition, and talent.

Each article in this book discusses a particular film occupation in detail. The articles in *Careers in Focus: Film* appear in Ferguson's *Encyclopedia of Careers and Vocational Guidance,* but have been updated and revised with the latest information from the U.S. Department of Labor, professional organizations, and other sources. The following paragraphs detail the sections and features that appear in the book.

The **Quick Facts** section provides a brief summary of the career including recommended school subjects, personal skills, work environment, minimum educational requirements, salary ranges, certification or licensing requirements, and employment outlook. This section also provides acronyms and identification numbers for the following government classification indexes: the Dictionary of Occupational Titles (DOT), the Guide for Occupational Exploration (GOE), the National Occupational Classification (NOC) Index, and the Occupational Information Network (O*NET)-Standard Occupational Classification System (SOC) index. The DOT, GOE, and O*NET-SOC indexes have been created by the U.S. government; the NOC index is Canada's career classification system. Readers can use the identification numbers listed in the Quick Facts section to access further information about a career. Print editions of the DOT (*Dictionary of Occupational Titles.* Indianapolis, Ind.: JIST Works, 1991) and GOE (*Guide for Occupational Exploration.* Indianapolis, Ind.: JIST Works, 2001) are available at libraries. Electronic versions of the DOT (http://www.oalj.dol.gov/libdot.htm), NOC (http://www5.hrsdc.gc.ca/NOC), and O*NET-SOC (http://www.onetonline.org) are available on the Internet. When no DOT, GOE, NOC, or O*NET-SOC numbers are listed, this means that the U.S. Department of Labor or Human Resources and Skills Development Canada have not created a numerical designation for this career. In this instance, you will see the acronym "N/A," or not available.

The **Overview** section is a brief introductory description of the duties and responsibilities involved in this career. Oftentimes, a career may have a variety of job titles. When this is the case, alternative career titles are presented. Employment statistics are also provided, when available. The **History** section describes the history of the particular job as it relates to the overall development of its industry or field. **The Job** describes the primary and secondary duties of the job. **Requirements** discusses high school and postsecondary education and training requirements, any certification or licensing that is necessary, and other personal requirements for success in the job. **Exploring** offers suggestions on how to gain experience in or knowledge of the particular job before making a firm educational and financial commitment. The focus is on what can be done while still in high school (or in the early years of college) to gain a better understanding of the job. The **Employers** section gives an overview of typical places of employment for the job. **Starting Out** discusses the best ways to land that first job, be it through the college career services office, newspaper ads, Internet employment sites, or personal contact. The **Advancement** section describes what kind of career path to expect from the job and how to get there. **Earnings** lists salary ranges and describes the typical fringe benefits. The **Work Environment** section describes the typical surroundings and conditions of employment—whether indoors or outdoors, noisy or quiet, social or independent. Also discussed are typical hours worked, any seasonal fluctuations, and the stresses and strains of the job. The **Outlook** section summarizes the job in terms of the general economy and industry projections. For the most part, Outlook information is obtained from the U.S. Bureau of Labor Statistics and is supplemented by information gathered from professional associations. Job growth terms follow those used in the *Occupational Outlook Handbook*. Growth described as "much faster than the average" means an increase of 20 percent or more. Growth described as "faster than the average" means an increase of 14 to 19 percent. Growth described as "about as fast as the average" means an increase of 7 to 13 percent. Growth described as "more slowly than the average" means an increase of 3 to 6 percent. "Little or no change" means a decrease of 2 percent to an increase of 2 percent. "Decline" means a decrease of 3 percent or more. Each article ends with **For More Information,** which lists organizations that provide information on training, education, internships, scholarships, and job placement.

Careers in Focus: Film also includes photos, informative sidebars, and interviews with professionals in the field.

Actors

OVERVIEW

Actors play parts or roles in dramatic productions in motion pictures, on the stage, or on television or radio. They impersonate, or portray, characters by speech, gesture, song, and dance. There are approximately 56,500 actors working in the United States.

HISTORY

Drama, which began as a component of religious festivals, was refined as an art form by the ancient Greeks, who used the stage as a forum for topical themes and stories. The role of actors became more important than in the past, and settings became more realistic with the use of scenery. Playgoing was often a great celebration, a tradition carried on by the Romans. The rise of the Christian church put an end to theater in the 6th century A.D., and for several centuries actors were ostracized from society, surviving as jugglers and jesters.

Drama was reintroduced during the Middle Ages but became more religious in focus. Plays during this period typically centered around biblical themes, and roles were played by craftspeople and other amateurs. This changed with the rediscovery of Greek and Roman plays in the Renaissance. Professional actors and acting troupes toured the countries of Europe, presenting ancient plays or improvising new dramas based on cultural issues and situations of the day. Actors began to take on more prominence in society. In England, actors such as Will Kemp and Richard Burbage became known for their roles in the plays of William Shakespeare. In France, Molière wrote and often acted in his own plays. Until the mid-17th century, however, women were banned from the stage, and young boys played the roles of women.

By the 18th century, actors could become quite prominent members of society, and plays were often written—or, in the case of Shakespeare's plays, rewritten—to suit a particular actor. Acting styles tended to be highly exaggerated, with elaborate gestures and artificial speech, until David Garrick introduced a more natural style to the stage in the mid-1700s. The first American acting company was established in Williamsburg, Virginia, in 1752, led by Lewis Hallan. In the next century, many actors became stars: famous actors of the time included Edwin Forrest, Fanny and Charles Kemble, Edmund Kean, William Charles Macready, and Joseph Jefferson, who was particularly well known for his comedic roles.

Until the late 19th century, stars dominated the stage. But in 1874, George II, Duke of Saxe-Meiningen, formed a theater troupe in which every actor was given equal prominence. This ensemble style influenced others, such as Andre Antoine of France, and gave rise to a new trend in theater called naturalism, which featured far more realistic characters in more realistic settings than before. This style of theater came to dominate the 20th century. It also called for new methods of acting. Konstantin Stanislavsky of the Moscow Art Theater, who developed an especially influential acting style that was later called method acting, influenced the Group Theater in the United States; one member, Lee Strasberg, founded The Actors Studio in New York, which would become an important training ground for many of the great American actors. In the early 20th century, vaudeville and burlesque shows were extremely popular and became the training ground for some of the great comic actors of the century.

By then, developments such as film, radio, and television offered many more acting opportunities than ever before. Many actors honed their skills on the stage and then entered one of these new media, where they could become known throughout the nation and often throughout the world. Both radio and television offered still more acting opportunities in advertisements. The development of sound in film caused many popular actors from the silent era to fade from view, while giving rise to many others. But almost from the beginning, film stars were known for their outrageous salaries and lavish style of living.

Hollywood is the recognized capital of the motion picture and television industries. Additionally, many movie and television production companies are located in New York City.

Actors Will Smith and Kevin James discuss a scene with director Andy Tennant on the set of *Hitch*. *(ColumbiaPictures/Topham/The Image Works)*

THE JOB

The imitation or basic development of a character for presentation to an audience often seems like a glamorous and fairly easy job. In reality, it is demanding, tiring work requiring a special talent.

The actor must first find a part available in some upcoming production. This may be in a comedy, drama, musical, or opera. Then, having read and studied the part, the actor must audition before the director and other people who have control of the production. This requirement is often waived for established artists. In film and television, actors must also complete screen tests, which are scenes recorded on film, at times performed with other actors, which are later viewed by the director and producer of the film or television show.

If selected for the part, the actor must spend many hours in rehearsal and must memorize many lines and cues. This is especially true in live theater; in film and television, actors may spend less time in rehearsal and sometimes improvise their lines before the camera, often performing several attempts, or "takes," before the director is satisfied.

In addition to such mechanical duties, the actor must determine the essence of the character being portrayed and the relation of that character to the overall scheme of the play. In many film and theater roles, actors must also sing and dance and spend additional time rehearsing songs and perfecting the choreography. Some roles require actors to perform various stunts, which can be quite dangerous. Most often, these stunts are performed by specially trained *stunt performers* (see the article Stunt Performers). Others work as *stand-ins* or *body doubles*. These actors are chosen for specific features and appear on film in place of the lead actor; this is often the case in films requiring nude or seminude scenes.

Actors in films may spend several weeks involved in a production, which often takes place on location, that is, in different parts of the world. They also work on movie sets, which are often located in Los Angeles and New York City—the major production hubs of the movie industry.

While studying and perfecting their craft, many actors work as *extras,* the nonspeaking characters that appear in the background on screen or stage. Many actors also continue their training. A great deal of an actor's time is spent attending auditions.

REQUIREMENTS

High School

There are no minimum educational requirements to become an actor. However, at least a high school diploma is recommended. In high school, take any drama classes that are offered and participate in theater clubs and productions.

Postsecondary Training

As acting becomes more and more involved with the various facets of our society, a college degree will become more important to those who hope to have an acting career. It is assumed that the actor who has completed a liberal arts program is more capable of understanding the wide variety of roles that are available. Therefore, it is strongly recommended that aspiring actors complete at least a bachelor's degree program in theater or the dramatic arts. In addition, graduate degrees in the fine arts or in drama are nearly always required should the individual decide to teach dramatic arts.

College can also provide acting experience for the hopeful actor. More than 500 colleges and universities throughout the country offer dramatic arts programs and present theatrical performances. Actors and directors recommend that those interested in acting gain as much experience as possible through acting in plays in high school and college or in those offered by community groups.

Other Requirements

Prospective actors will be required not only to have a great talent for acting but also a great determination to succeed. They must be able to memorize hundreds of lines and should have a good speaking voice. The ability to sing and dance is important for increasing the opportunities for the young actor. Almost all actors, even the biggest stars, are required to audition for a part before they receive the role. In film and television, they will generally complete screen tests to see how they will appear on film. In all fields of acting, a love for acting is a must. It might take many years for an actor to achieve any success, if at all.

While union membership may not always be required, many actors find it advantageous to belong to a union that covers their particular field of performing arts. These organizations include the Actors' Equity Association (stage), Screen Actors Guild (motion pictures and television films), or American Federation of Television and Radio Artists (TV, recording, and radio). In addition, some actors may benefit from membership in the American Guild of Variety Artists (nightclubs, and so on), American Guild of Musical Artists (opera and ballet), or organizations such as the Guild of Italian American Actors.

EXPLORING

The best way to explore this career is to participate in school or local theater productions. Even working on the props or lighting crew will provide insight into the field.

Also, attend as many dramatic productions as possible and try to talk with people who either are currently in the theater or have been at one time. They can offer advice to individuals interested in a career in the theater.

Many books have been written about acting, not only concerning how to perform but also about the nature of the work, its offerings, advantages, and disadvantages. Ask your school or local librarian to suggest some titles.

Finally, ask your drama teacher or a school counselor to arrange an information interview with an actor.

EMPLOYERS

Approximately 56,500 actors are employed in the United States. Motion pictures, television, and the stage are the largest fields of employment for actors, with television commercials representing as much as 60 percent of all acting jobs. Most of the opportunities for employment in these fields are either in Los Angeles or in New York.

As cable television networks continue to produce more and more of their own programs and films, they will become a major provider of employment for actors. The music video business and the growth of the Internet will also continue to create new acting jobs.

The lowest numbers of actors are employed for stage work. In addition to Broadway shows and regional theater, there are employment opportunities for stage actors in summer stock, at resorts, and on cruise ships.

STARTING OUT

Probably the best way to enter acting is to start with high school, local, or college productions and to gain as much experience as possible on that level. Very rarely is an inexperienced actor given an opportunity to perform on stage or in a film production in New York or Hollywood. The field is extremely difficult to enter; the more experience and ability beginners have, however, the greater the possibilities for entrance.

Those venturing to New York or Hollywood are encouraged first to have enough money to support themselves during the long waiting and searching period normally required before a job is found. Most will list themselves with a casting agency that will help them find a part as an extra or a bit player, either in theater or film. These agencies keep names on file along with photographs and a description of the individual's features and experience, and if a part comes along that may be suitable, they contact that person. Very often, however, names are added to their lists only when the number of people in a particular physical category is low. For instance, the agency may not have enough athletic young women on their roster, and if the applicant happens to fit this description, her name is added.

To learn more about breaking into this career, you might also consider visiting the Screen Actors Guild's Web site (http://www.sag .org/content/getting-started-actor-faq) to read the online publication *Getting Started as an Actor.*

ADVANCEMENT

New actors will normally start in bit parts and will have only a few lines to speak, if any. The normal procession of advancement would then lead to larger supporting roles. Many film and television actors get their start in commercials or by appearing in government and commercially sponsored public service announcements, films, and programs. Other actors join the afternoon soap operas on television and continue on to evening programs. Many actors have also gotten their start in on-camera roles such as presenting the weather segment of a local news program. Once an actor has gained experience, he or she may go on to play stronger supporting roles or even leading roles in stage, television, or film productions. From there, an actor may go on to stardom. Only a very small number of actors ever reach that pinnacle, however.

Some actors eventually go into other, related occupations and become drama coaches, drama teachers, producers, stage directors, motion picture directors, television directors, radio directors, stage managers, casting directors, or artist and repertoire managers. Others may combine one or more of these functions while continuing their career as an actor.

EARNINGS

The wage scale for actors is largely controlled through bargaining agreements reached by various unions in negotiations with producers. These agreements normally control the minimum salaries, hours of work permitted per week, and other conditions of employment. In addition, each artist enters into a separate contract that may provide for higher salaries.

In 2010, the minimum daily salary of any member of the Screen Actors Guild (SAG) in a speaking role was $809 or $4,045 for a five-day workweek. Motion picture actors may also receive additional payments known as residuals as part of their guaranteed salary. Many actors receive residuals whenever films, TV shows, and TV commercials in which they appear are rerun, sold for TV exhibition, or put on DVD or offered for download online. Residuals often exceed the actors' original salary and account for about one-third of all actors' income.

According to the U.S. Department of Labor (DOL), the median yearly earnings of actors employed in the motion picture and video industries were $99,216 in 2009. The department also reported the lowest paid 10 percent of all actors earned less than $16,598.

The annual earnings of persons in movies are affected by frequent periods of unemployment. Unions offer health, welfare, and pension funds for members working over a set number of weeks a year. Some actors are eligible for paid vacation and sick time, depending on the work contract.

In all fields, well-known actors have salary rates far above the minimums, and the salaries of the few top stars are many times higher. In film, top stars may earn more than $20 million per film, and, after receiving a percentage of the gross earned by the film, these stars can earn far, far more.

A number of actors cannot receive unemployment compensation when they are waiting for their next part, primarily because they have not worked enough to meet the minimum eligibility requirements for compensation. Sick leaves and paid vacations are not usually available to the actor. However, union actors who earn the minimum qualifications now receive full medical and health insurance under all the actors' unions. Those who earn health plan benefits for 10 years become eligible for a pension upon retirement. The acting field is very uncertain. Aspirants never know whether they will be able to get into the profession, and, once in, there are uncertainties as to whether the show will be well received and, if not, whether the actors' talent can survive a bad show.

WORK ENVIRONMENT

Actors employed in motion pictures may work in air-conditioned studios one week and be on location in a hot desert the next. They may be required to work 12- to 16-hour days to meet production deadlines. The work can sometimes be stressful, especially if filming takes the actor away from his or her family for long periods of time. On the other hand, many actors enjoy the fame and notoriety that comes with a successful acting career.

OUTLOOK

Employment for actors who work in the motion picture and video industries is expected to grow about as fast as the average for all careers through 2018, according to the DOL. The growth of satellite and cable television in the past decade has created a demand for more actors, especially as the cable networks produce more and more of their own programs and films. The rise of home entertainment options (such as direct-for-Web movies, mobile content produced for cell phones or other portable electronic devices, and DVD and online rentals) has also created new acting jobs, as more and more films are made strictly for the home market.

There are also opportunities for actors in theater. Many resorts built in the 1980s and 1990s present their own theatrical productions, providing more job opportunities for actors. Jobs in theater, however, face pressure as the cost of mounting a production rises and as many nonprofit and smaller theaters lose their funding.

Despite the growth in opportunities, there are many more actors than there are roles, and this is likely to remain true for years to come. This is true in all areas of the arts, including radio, television, motion pictures, and theater, and even those who are normally employed during only a small portion of the year. Many actors must supplement their income by working at other jobs, such as secretaries, waiters, or taxi drivers, for example. Almost all performers are members of more than one union in order to take advantage of various opportunities as they become available.

It should be recognized that of the 56,500 or so actors in the United States today, only a small percentage are working as actors at any one time. Of these, few are able to support themselves on their earnings from acting, and fewer still will ever achieve stardom. Most actors work for many years before becoming known, and most of these do not rise above supporting roles. The vast majority of actors, meanwhile, are still looking for the right break. There are many more applicants in all areas than there are positions. As with most careers in the arts, people enter this career out of a love and desire for acting.

FOR MORE INFORMATION

The following is a professional union for actors in theater and "live" industrial productions, stage managers, some directors, and choreographers:

Actors' Equity Association
165 West 46th Street
New York, NY 10036-2500
Tel: 212-869-8530
http://www.actorsequity.org

This union represents television and radio performers, including actors, announcers, dancers, disc jockeys, newspersons, singers, specialty acts, sportscasters, and stuntpersons.

American Federation of Television and Radio Artists
260 Madison Avenue
New York, NY 10016-2401
Tel: 212-532-0800
http://www.aftra.com

The International Thespian Society is the student division of the Educational Theatre Association. It is the largest honor society for theater arts students in the world. It has clubs at more than 3,600 affiliated schools in the United States, Canada, and other countries. Students in grades six through 12 are eligible to be inducted into the society. Students can participate in the International Thespian Festival, an "educational and performance event for middle and high school theatre . . . which features a variety of performances from some of the best high school theatre programs, hands-on workshops, auditions for the National Individual Events Showcase, and scholarship and college auditions."

International Thespian Society
c/o Educational Theatre Association
2343 Auburn Avenue
Cincinnati, OH 45219-2815
Tel: 513-421-3900
http://schooltheatre.org/society

For answers to a number of frequently asked questions concerning education, visit the NAST Web site.

National Association of Schools of Theatre (NAST)
11250 Roger Bacon Drive, Suite 21
Reston, VA 20190-5248
Tel: 703-437-0700
E-mail: info@arts-accredit.org
http://nast.arts-accredit.org

This union represents film and television performers. It offers general information on actors, directors, and producers.

Screen Actors Guild
5757 Wilshire Boulevard, 7th Floor
Los Angeles, CA 90036-3600
Tel: 323-954-1600
http://www.sag.org

For information on theatrical careers, contact

Theatre Communications Group
520 Eighth Avenue, 24th Floor
New York, NY 10018-4156
Tel: 212-609-5900
E-mail: tcg@tcg.org
http://www.tcg.org

This site has information for beginners on acting and the acting business.

Acting Workshop On-Line
http://www.redbirdstudio.com/AWOL/acting2.html

INTERVIEW

Dexter Bullard is the head of the Graduate Acting Program, teaches in the Undergraduate Acting Program, and serves as the Showcase Season artistic director at The Theatre School at DePaul University in Chicago, Illinois. He is also an award-winning theatrical director. In 2004, Dexter was awarded the Lucille Lortel Award for Outstanding Direction Off-Broadway for Tracy Letts' Bug *at the Barrow Street Theater, as well as a Drama Desk Nomination for Outstanding Director. He discussed the field of acting and DePaul's undergraduate acting program with the editors of* Careers in Focus: Film.

Q. What are a few things that young people may not know about a career in acting?

A. One thing young people may not know is that a career in acting involves a lot of interpersonal relationships. A career in acting means you need to know, and get along, with a great number of people. This is true for so many other businesses and careers, but so much more in acting, because this field is based on opportunities. The most important skill for an actor, besides the ability to act, of course, is being able to put him/herself in different situations to find these opportunities. This means—knowing what's going on, knowing who is reliable, and knowing yourself and what you have to offer. Being successful means having a relationship with yourself that you either manage well, or you don't. People may not realize how much time it takes to establish oneself as an actor and how much joy there is in this career.

Making and maintaining contacts in this field is so important. So many times I found opportunities because of somebody who pulled me along on something. We attach each other to things; we build trust.

So many parents think a career in acting means you're a waiter, or you're a celebrity. But there is a middle ground and such satisfaction in working in the arts. The people who work in this industry are terrific. Not everything we do is for the chase of money. Some of the things we do are for the interaction with other human beings and the chance to make a difference in life through participation in the performing arts.

I personally know hundreds, if not thousands, of theater people who are not making all of their living just by being on stage or in movies. But they are making part of their living by being in the theater or being around it—and still being creative people.

Q. What are the most important personal and professional qualities for acting students?

A. Emotional honesty is critical for actors. Teens, especially, are very emotional creatures, but not always in touch with how they can express these emotions. A certain level of maturity can help you assess why you have these feelings. A lot of teenagers can try to rely on being cute and generally relaxed with different situations on stage or film. But what is really wanted is one who can put themselves in the given circumstance and can feel things that move the scenes and moments. With being truly involved, they can be honest and capture an audience. This is an art form, and not just a hobby.

In theater, you need a lot of discipline, of course. Acting is not a job for which you can be late.

Q. Is life experience important for gaining maturity on stage or in film?

A. Not so much. There are a lot of ways that level of maturity comes to people. Some are born with it; some have the sense of knowing what their feelings are. They are able to open themselves up and let others know what their feelings are, and not necessarily in a touchy, feely way. Al Pacino knows what his feelings are, and he's definitely not "touchy feely." I'm talking about a candidness and openness. Definitely this can happen with training—we do a lot on this topic within our program at The Theatre School. This training can help actors with roles in different circumstances. You don't need a lot of life experience, but you will have to borrow from a lot of places in your life.

Q. What are the most important professional qualities for actors?

A. You need to be a good communicator—regardless if you are communicating in a given circumstances, or a communicator in a room (full of people). Actors need to be able to use expressions—body and voice—along with their charisma and presence—to move people. Communication is something that can be taught. People have a certain communication set. They've learned this through their parents, cultural context, peers, and personal identity. There is a huge range of people who can be actors. It's all about being someone who is responsive, open, really listening, and forward—someone who is not hiding.

It's not about shyness—there are some great actors who have inhibitions. It's also not about being an extrovert. It's about knowing when it's time to communicate. Some of the best acting students I have are actually quite shy. We all put off a signal, and going to school is about finding out about our signal—how do I put out a good signal? A clear signal. A great part of our training has to do with becoming aware of how we sound, move, speak, and respond. After four years you have a person who is more aware, more confident, and more relaxed.

Q. Can you provide an overview of the undergraduate acting program at DePaul?

A. The four-year B.F.A. in acting program is an intense immersion into all disciplines of performance. Starting with a base of voice, movement, scene study and improvisation—our actors' work becomes broader in range, and their artistic tools are shaped and honed as they continue their studies.

We start with a certain number of students during the first year, the probationary year. This is when students find out if the school is right for them, and vice versa. The second year, we bring back a smaller core of students who really want to dig deeper into this program and future careers. Our approach is strictly nonscript based the first year. We are known for our use of improv, acting exercises, and prescenic techniques. Chicago is known for building an actor who is not just someone who interprets literature, but is someone who has learned different kinds of communication skills and scenic skills—all the things that come before a script.

Our program is very competitive. We bring in about 42 students in the first year, and bring back about 26 for the second year. DePaul's is one of the few programs with an invitation to return policy. The reason for this is that we want our class sizes to be small, and we want our investment to be conservatory [in] style. We also guarantee casting. If you make it into the second year, you are going to be in nine productions for the next three years. We are going to make sure you are trained in lead roles and in supporting roles—in all types of spaces. We are also a full-spectrum theater school—not just an acting school. You'll be working with designers, writers, and directors—we teach everything that has to do with theater.

Q. What is the future of your program?

A. The future of our program is always the students, alumni, faculty, and staff. Their professional work continues the work of the school on a nationwide basis. Also, I know we're in the process of getting new facilities—that is probably going to be the biggest change to the program. New theater, new classes, new building. We're doing more and more things with technology. We're bringing students into different places, especially with casting. We're helping put actors' work online, finding ways to get their work out there. We are getting away from the old way of thinking about theater, and finding new ways of thinking. The number one thing we are bringing out in our program is entrepreneurial spirit. We give students inspiration and tools to bring out their own work, make their own choices, and bring themselves into the community—making things happen.

Q. What has been one of your rewarding experiences as an educator?

A. As an educator, I would have to say it's when I meet a former student of mine working in the world. While I was the teacher at Theatre School, that student listened to me; out in the acting world, it's me listening to them. It's at this time that I'm reminded that they were an artist all along and have found the courage to get involved beyond school.

Animators

OVERVIEW

Animators are artists who design the moving characters that appear in movies, television shows, and commercials. Approximately 7,720 animators and multimedia artists are employed in the motion picture and video industries.

HISTORY

Frenchmen Emile Reynaud created what is considered the first animated cartoon in 1892. He created the cartoon by drawing and hand-painting images on film paper and using a praxinoscope, an optical instrument he invented to create the illusion of movement, or animation. *Fantasmagorie,* considered the first fully animated film, was made by French director Emile Courtet (aka Emile Cohl) in 1908.

As Hollywood grew in the early 1900s, so did companies that created cartoons, although these animated films were silent (just like all movies of the time). Bray Studios in New York City was one of the best-known cartoon studios of the time. It operated from circa 1915 to the late 1920s. Some of its cartoons include *Out of the Inkwell* (1916), *Electric Bell* (1918), and *If You Could Shrink* (1920).

Walt Disney also got his start in the business around this time. In 1923, he sold his first cartoon, *Alice's Wonderland,* to a distributor and soon after founded Disney Brothers Cartoon Studio (later renamed Walt Disney Studio) with his brother, Roy. By the late 1920s "talkies" had replaced silent films and Walt Disney had created the cartoon character, Mickey Mouse, which still entertains young and old to this day.

QUICK FACTS

School Subjects
Art
Computer science

Personal Skills
Artistic
Communication/ideas

Work Environment
Primarily indoors
Primarily one location

Minimum Education Level
High school diploma

Salary Range
$32,360 to $70,960 to $99,130+

Certification or Licensing
None available

Outlook
Much faster than the average

DOT
141

GOE
01.04.02

NOC
5241

O*NET-SOC
27–1014.00

The 1930s and 1940s are considered the golden age of animation. The Walt Disney Studio dominated the industry during these decades. During this time, it created the first animated feature film, *Snow White and the Seven Dwarfs*, which debuted in 1937. The animated film was so groundbreaking that the Academy of Motion Pictures and Sciences gave it a special award in 1938, stating: "to Walt Disney for *Snow White and the Seven Dwarfs*, recognized as a significant screen innovation which has charmed millions and pioneered a great new entertainment field for the motion picture cartoon." Walt Disney Studio went on to create many other animated feature-length classics, including *Pinocchio, Fantasia*, and *Dumbo*.

The popularity of television in the 1950s caused a decline in interest in theatrical cartoons and feature films that lasted into the 1980s. Many consider the release of *Who Framed Roger Rabbit?* by Walt Disney Studios in 1988 as the beginning of a renaissance in film animation that continues to this day. Major animation trends over the last two decades include the popularity of adult-oriented animation, such as *Waltz with Bashir* and television shows such as *The Simpsons, Family Guy*, and *South Park;* the emergence of anime [Japanese-based (although the phenomena has spread throughout Asia) high- quality animation in a variety of genres that is geared not just toward children, but adults, too]; the creation of cable networks, such as Nickelodeon and the Cartoon Network, that offer animation as much or all of their programming; and the rise of computer-generated animation, which allows animators infinite creative options and the ability to complete animated features in far less time than by using traditional methods.

THE JOB

Animators, sometimes called *motion cartoonists*, design the moving characters that appear in films and television shows. They also create the visual effects for many films, television shows, and commercials. Making a big budget animated film, such as *WALL-E, Ratatouille, A Bug's Life*, or *Shrek*, requires a team of many creative people. Each animator on the team works on one small part of the film. On a small production, animators may be involved in many different aspects of the project's development.

An animated film begins with a script. *Screenwriters* plan the story line, or plot, and write it with dialogue and narration. *Designers* read the script and decide how the film should look—should it be realistic, futuristic, or humorous? They then draw some of the

Useful Web Sites for Animators

Animated Views
http://animatedviews.com

Animation Insider
http://www.animationinsider.net

Animation Magazine
http://www.animationmagazine.net

AnimationMentor.com
http://animationmentor.com

Animation World Network
http://www.awn.com

The Big Cartoon Database
http://www.bcdb.com

Chuck Jones
http://www.chuckjones.com

DreamWorks Animation
http://www.dreamworksanimation.com

Pixar
http://www.pixar.com

StopMotionAnimation.com
http://www.stopmotionanimation.com

The Walt Disney Family Museum
http://disney.go.com/disneyatoz/familymuseum

characters and backgrounds. These designs are then passed on to a *storyboard artist* who illustrates the whole film in a series of frames, similar to a very long comic strip. Based on this storyboard, an artist can then create a detailed layout.

In the past, the most common form of animation was cel animation, in which animators drew the artwork on cels and then prepared the finished film frame by frame, or cel by cel. Today, most animators forego creating on cels (except in planning stages) and instead use computer software to draw directly into a computer system. Computer programs can create effects like shadows, reflections, distortions, and dissolves. Animators are relying increasingly on computers in various areas of production. Computers are used to color animation art, whereas formerly, every frame was painted by hand. Computers also help animators create special effects and even entire films. (One animation software program, Macromedia's Flash, has given rise to an entire Internet cartoon subculture.)

Stop-motion animation is a traditional animation form that is still popular today. In stop-motion animation, an object, such as a doll, is photographed, moved slightly, and photographed again. The process is repeated hundreds of thousands of times to make a film. Movies, such as *Chicken Run,* were animated this way. Claymation is one of the most common forms of stop-motion animation and was popularized by the *Gumby* animated series. Using this approach, the objects being photographed are made of clay.

REQUIREMENTS

High School

If you are interested in becoming an animator, you should, of course, take art as well as computer classes in high school. Math classes, such as algebra and geometry, will also be helpful. If your school

Animators Trey Parker and Matt Stone work with marionettes on the set of *Team America: World Police. (Topham/The Image Works)*

offers graphic design and computer animation classes, be sure to take those.

Postsecondary Training

You do not need to go to college to become an animator, but many colleges are beginning to offer classes and degrees in computer animation, digital art, computer and video game design, and related fields. Some of today's top computer animators are self-taught or have learned their skills on the job, but as competition for jobs increases, it is a good idea to earn at least an associate's degree in animation or a related field.

In addition to formal training, you should learn as many software programs as possible such as Maya, Photoshop, Final Cut, Premiere, and After Effects.

Other Requirements

Animators must be creative. In addition to having artistic talent, they must generate ideas, although it is not unusual for animators to collaborate with writers for ideas. They must have a good sense of humor (or a good dramatic sense) and an observant eye to detect people's distinguishing characteristics and society's interesting attributes or incongruities.

Animators need to be flexible. Because their art is commercial, they must be willing to accommodate their employers' desires if they are to build a broad clientele and earn a decent living. They must be able to take suggestions and rejections gracefully.

You should also have extensive knowledge of animation software and be willing to continue to learn throughout your career since animation and computer technology changes almost constantly.

EXPLORING

Ask your high school art or computer science teacher to arrange a presentation by an animator, or if you live near an animation studio, try to arrange a tour of a production facility. Sketch as much as you possibly can. Carry a sketchpad around in order to quickly capture images and gestures that seem interesting to you. There are many computer animation software programs available that teach basic principles and techniques. Experiment with these programs to create basic animation. Some video cameras have stop-motion buttons that allow you to take a series of still shots. You can use this feature to experiment with claymation and other stop-motion techniques.

EMPLOYERS

Approximately 7,720 animators and multimedia artists are employed in the motion picture and video industries. Employers of animators include producers, movie studios, television production companies, and computer and video game design firms. In addition, a number of these artists are self-employed, working on a freelance basis. Some do animation on the Web as a part-time business or a hobby.

STARTING OUT

Larger employers, such as Pixar, offer apprenticeships or internships. To enter these programs, applicants must be attending a college animation program. Interns at Pixar must have completed their junior year of college, be a current graduate student, or have graduated during the year the internship begins. Program participants might work as camera and staging artist interns, who "create sequences of shots that convey the story through the application of traditional filmmaking principles in a 3D computer graphics environment." Other internship options at Pixar are available in technical direction, production management, story, marketing, engineering and editorial.

Volunteering with a local animation or film production company is the next best thing to landing an internship. This experience will give you a great introduction to the field and help you to make valuable contacts in the field.

One new way up-and-coming animators have made themselves known to the animating community is by attracting an audience on the World Wide Web. A portfolio of well-executed Web 'toons can help an animator build his reputation and get jobs. Some animators, such as The Brothers Chaps (creators of http://www.homestarrunner.com), have even been able to turn their creations into a profitable business.

ADVANCEMENT

Animators' success, like that of other artists, depends on how much the public likes their work. Very successful animators work for well-known film companies and other employers at the best wages; some become well known to the public.

EARNINGS

According to the U.S. Department of Labor (DOL), multimedia artists and animators who were employed in the motion picture and video industries earned an annual mean salary of $70,960 in 2009. Salaries for all multimedia artists and animators ranged from less than $32,360 to more than $99,130.

Self-employed artists do not receive fringe benefits such as paid vacations, sick leave, health insurance, or pension benefits. Those who are salaried employees of companies and the like do typically receive these fringe benefits.

WORK ENVIRONMENT

Most animators work in big cities where movie and television studios are located. They generally work in comfortable environments with good lighting and the latest computer technology. Staff animators work a regular 40-hour workweek but may occasionally be expected to work evenings and weekends to meet deadlines. Freelance animators have erratic schedules, and the number of hours they work may depend on how much money they want to earn or how much work they can find. They often work evenings and weekends but are not required to be at work during regular office hours.

Animators can be frustrated by employers who curtail their creativity, asking them to follow instructions that are contrary to what they would most like to do. Many freelance animators spend a lot of time working alone at home, but animators have more opportunities to interact with other people than do most working artists.

OUTLOOK

Employment for animators and multimedia artists who work in the motion picture and video industries is expected to grow much faster than the average for all careers through 2018, according to the DOL. The growing trend of sophisticated special effects in motion pictures should create opportunities at industry effects houses such as Sony Pictures Imageworks, DreamQuest Software, Industrial Light & Magic, and DreamWorks SKG. Furthermore, growing processor and Internet connection speeds have created an animation renaissance. Demand is also increasing as animation is increasingly used in mobile technologies and in nonentertainment-based fields such as scientific research or design services. Because so many creative and talented people are drawn to this field, however, competition for jobs will be strong.

Animated features are not just for children anymore. Much of the animation today is geared for an adult audience. Interactive computer games, animated films, network and cable television, and the Internet are among the many employment sources for talented animators. About 60 percent of all visual artists are self-employed, but freelance work can be hard to come by, and many freelancers earn little until they acquire experience and establish a good reputation. Competition for work will be keen; those with an undergraduate or advanced degree in animation, art, or film will be in demand. Experience in action drawing and computers is a must.

FOR MORE INFORMATION

For information about animated films and digital effects, visit the AWN Web site, which includes feature articles, a list of schools, and a career section.

Animation World Network (AWN)
6525 Sunset Boulevard, Garden Suite 10
Hollywood, CA 90028-7212
Tel: 323-606-4200
E-mail: info@awn.com
http://www.awn.com

The guild represents the interests of animation professionals in California. Visit its Web site for information on training, earnings, and the animation industry.

Animators Guild Local 839
1105 North Hollywood Way
Burbank, CA 91505-2528
Tel: 818-845-7500
E-mail: info@animationguild.org
http://animationguild.org

For membership and scholarship information, contact
International Animated Film Society-ASIFA Hollywood
2114 West Burbank Boulevard
Burbank, CA 91506-1232
Tel: 818-842-4691
E-mail: info@asifa-hollywood.org
http://www.asifa-hollywood.org

For an art school directory and general information, contact
National Art Education Association
1806 Robert Fulton Drive, Suite 300
Reston, VA 20191-4348
Tel: 703-860-8000
E-mail: info@arteducators.org
http://www.arteducators.org

Visit the society's Web site for information about festivals and pre-sentations and news about the industry.

Visual Effects Society
5535 Balboa Boulevard, Suite 205
Encino, CA 91316-1544
Tel: 818-981-7861
E-mail: info@visualeffectssociety.com
http://www.visualeffectssociety.com

This nonprofit organization represents the professional interests of women (and men) in animation. Visit its Web site for industry information, links to animation blogs, details on membership for high school students, and its quarterly newsletter.

Women in Animation
E-mail: wia@womeninanimation.org
http://wia.animationblogspot.com

Cinematographers and Directors of Photography

OVERVIEW

The *cinematographer*, also known as the *director of photography (DP)*, is instrumental in establishing the mood of a film by putting the narrative aspects of a script into visual form. The cinematographer is responsible for every shot's framing, lighting, color level, and exposure elements that set the artistic tone of a film. Approximately 5,400 cinematographers are employed in the motion picture and video industries.

HISTORY

Motion picture cameras were invented in the late 1800s. In 1903, Edwin Porter made *The Great Train Robbery*, the first motion picture that used modern filmmaking techniques to tell a story. Porter filmed the scenes out of sequence, then edited and put them together to make the film, as is done today.

In the early years of film, the director handled the camera and made the artistic decisions that today are the job of the director of photography. The technical sophistication and artistic choices that are part of today's filming process had not yet emerged; instead, directors merely filmed narratives without moving the camera. Lighting was more for functional purposes of illumination than for artistic effect. Soon, however, directors began to experiment. They moved the camera to shoot from different angles and established a variety of editing techniques.

Learn More About It: Film Education

Edgar, Tom, and Karin Kelly. *Film School Confidential: The Insider's Guide to Film Schools.* New York: Perigee Trade, 2007.

Landau, Neil, and Matthew Frederick. *101 Things I Learned in Film School.* Boston: Grand Central Publishing, 2010.

National Association of Schools of Theatre. *National Association of Schools of Theatre Directory.* Reston, Va.: National Association of Schools of Theatre, 2008.

The Princeton Review. *Television, Film, and Digital Media Programs: 556 Outstanding Programs at Top Colleges and Universities Across the Nation.* New York: The Princeton Review, 2006.

In the 1950s, the dominance of major studios in film production was curbed by an antitrust court decision, and more independent films were made. Changes in the U.S. tax code made independent producing more profitable. New genres and trends challenged the director and artistic staff of a production. Science fiction, adventure, mystery, and romance films grew in popularity. By the late 1960s, university film schools were established to train students in directing and cinematography as well as in other areas.

New developments in technologies and equipment have continued to influence both how films are made and how they look. The end of the 20th century and the beginning of the 21st saw the production of movies incorporating such elements as computer graphics, digital imaging, digital color, and 3-D technology. Films such as *Titanic, Gladiator, Lord of the Rings,* and *Avatar* presented new visual challenges to filmmakers in terms of the amount and complexity of special and visual effects needed in the films. DPs have lead the way in understanding and using new technologies to push the art of filmmaking into the new, digital era.

THE JOB

Cinematographers consider how the look of a film helps to tell its story. How can the look enhance the action, the emotions expressed, or the characters' personalities? Should the scene be filmed from across the room or up close to the actors? Should the lighting be stark or muted? How does the angle of the camera contribute to the scene? These are just some of the questions DPs must answer when composing a shot. Because DPs have both artistic and technical knowledge, they are integral members of the production team. They work in both film and television, helping directors to interpret a script and bring it to life.

At the beginning of a project, the DP reads the script and talks to the director about how to film each scene. Together they determine how to achieve the desired effects by deciding on camera angles and movement, lighting, framing, and which filters to use. By manipulating effects, DPs help determine the mood of a scene. For example, to raise the level of tension and discomfort in an argument, the DP can tell a camera operator to film at an unusual angle or move around the actors as they speak. The director may choose to film a scene in more than one way and then decide which best suits the project. With good collaboration between the director and the DP, decisions will be made quickly and successfully.

DPs are responsible for assembling the camera crew and telling crew members how to film each scene. They must be knowledgeable about all aspects of camera operation, lighting, filters, and types of film. There are multiple ways an effect can be approached, and DPs must be aware of them in order to make suggestions to the director and to capture the mood desired.

For small, low-budget films, some of the crew's roles may be combined. For example, the DP may operate a camera in addition to overseeing the crew. In a large production, the crew's roles will be more specialized. The *camera operator* either operates the camera physically or controls it remotely, using a control panel. The *first assistant camera operator* helps with focus, changes lenses and filters, sets the stop for film exposure, and makes sure the camera is working properly. Camera focus is extremely important and is not judged simply by how the shot looks to the eye. Instead, the first assistant carries a measuring tape and measures all the key positions of the actors and makes calculations to ensure correct focus. The *second assistant camera operator,* also called the *loader,* loads film magazines, keeps track of how much film stock is left, and keeps camera reports. Camera reports record which shots the director likes and wants to have printed. A *gaffer* leads the electrical crew, and the grips handle the dollies and cranes to move the cameras.

When shooting begins, cinematographers take a series of test shots of film locations to determine the lighting, lenses, and film stock that will work best. Once filming starts, they make adjustments as necessary. They may also film screen tests of actors so the director can be sure they are right for their parts.

A director of photography (center) sets up a camera angle in preparation for filming. *(Rick Gebhard, AP Photo/*The Eagle Herald*)*

REQUIREMENTS

High School

To prepare for a career in cinematography, you should take college preparatory courses such as math, English, government, and foreign language. Courses in English composition and literature will give you a background in narrative development, and art and photography courses can help you understand the basics of lighting and composition. A broadcast journalism or media course may give you some hands-on experience in camera operation and video production.

Postsecondary Training

A bachelor's degree in liberal arts or film studies provides a good background for work in the film industry, but practical experience and industry connections will provide the best job opportunities. Upon completing an undergraduate program, you may wish to enroll in a master's program or master of fine arts program at a film school. Schools offering well-established programs include the School of Visual Arts in New York, New York University, and the University of Southern California. These schools have film professionals on their faculties and provide a very visible stage for student talent. In addition to classroom time, film school offers students the opportunity to work on their own productions. Such education is rigorous, but in addition to teaching skills it encourages peer groups and creates a network of contacts among students, faculty, and guest speakers that can be useful after graduation.

An alternative to film school is the New York Film Academy (NYFA). NYFA gives students an idea of the demands of filmmaking careers by immersing them in short, but intensive, workshops. During this time, students have access to cameras and editing tables and are required to make short films of their own. (Contact information for all schools is listed at the end of this article.)

Other Requirements

You'll need to keep abreast of technological innovations while working in the industry. You must be comfortable with the technical as well as artistic aspects of the profession. You also must be a good leader to make decisions and direct your crew effectively.

EXPLORING

With cable television, videos, the Internet, and DVDs, it is much easier to study films today than it was 25 years ago. Take full advantage of the availability of great films and study them closely for different filmmaking styles. The documentary *Visions of Light: The Art of Cinematography* (1992), directed by Arnold Glassman, Todd McCarthy, and Stuart Samuels, is a good introduction to some of the finest cinematography in the history of film. You can also experiment with composition and lighting if you have access to a 16-millimeter camera, a camcorder, or a digital camera. Check with your school's media center or journalism department about recording school events. Your school's drama club can also introduce you to the elements of comedy and drama and may involve you with writing and staging your own productions.

Subscribe to *American Cinematographer* magazine or read selected articles at the magazine's website (http://www.theasc.com/magazine). Other industry magazines such as *ICG Magazine* (http://www.icgmagazine.com/wordpress), *Daily Variety* (http://www.variety.com), *The Hollywood Reporter* (http://www.hollywoodreporter.com), and *Cinefex* (http://www.cinefex.com) can also give you insight into filmmaking.

EMPLOYERS

Approximately 5,400 cinematographers are employed in the motion picture and video industries. Motion picture studios, production companies, independent producers, and documentary filmmakers all employ DPs, either as salaried employees or as freelancers. Most freelancers are responsible for finding their own projects to work on, but a few are represented by agents who solicit work for them.

STARTING OUT

Internships are a very good way to gain experience and help you to become a marketable job candidate. Since local television stations and lower budget film productions operate with limited funds, they may offer internships for course credit or experience instead of a salary. You should check with your state's film commission to learn of productions in your area and volunteer to work in any capacity. Many production opportunities are also posted on the Web. By working on productions, you'll develop relationships with crew members and production assistants, and you'll be able to build a network of industry connections.

Before working as a DP, you'll likely work as a camera assistant or production assistant. To prepare yourself for this work, try to gain some experience in camera work with a college broadcasting station, a local TV crew, or advertising agency.

Cinematographers may choose to join a union because some film studios will hire only union members. The principal union for this field is the International Cinematographers Guild. Union members work under a union contract that determines their work rules, pay, and benefits.

ADVANCEMENT

The position of cinematographer is in itself an advanced position. Those wanting to work as cinematographers must work their way up the career ladder from first assistant camera operator, to camera operator, to DP.

Camera operators may have opportunities to work as cinematographers on some projects. As they continue to develop relationships with filmmakers and producers, their DP work may increase, leading to better paying, high-profile film projects. Once a DP has begun working in the industry, advancement may come as the DP develops a reputation for excellent, innovative work. Directors and producers may then request to work with that particular DP, which can also lead to higher pay.

EARNINGS

Many DPs do freelance work or have jobs under union contracts. They may work for a variety of employers ranging from major studios producing films with multimillion-dollar budgets to small, independent producers who are financing a film with their credit cards. As a result, their earnings vary widely.

When starting out as a camera operator, an individual may volunteer for a job, without pay, simply to get experience. At the other end of the earnings scale, a well-established DP working on big-budget productions can make well over $1 million a year. IATSE establishes minimum wage scales for DPs who are union members, based on the nature of a film shoot. Special provisions for holiday and overtime work are also made.

The U.S. Department of Labor (DOL), which categorizes DPs with all camera operators, reports the mean annual earnings for camera operators employed in the motion picture and video industries were $52,440 in 2009. The lowest paid 10 percent of all camera operators made less than $20,910. At the high end, 10 percent earned more than $82,600.

Freelancers must pay for their own benefits, such as health insurance, and they usually must buy their own equipment, which can be quite expensive.

WORK ENVIRONMENT

Conditions of work will vary depending on the size and nature of the production. In television production and in movies, DPs may work both indoors and outdoors. Indoors, conditions can be cramped, while outdoors there may be heat, cold, rain, or snow. DPs may need to travel for weeks at a time while a project is being shot on location, and some locations, such as the middle of a desert, may mean staying miles from civilization. Hours can be long and the shooting schedule rigorous, especially when a film is going over budget. DPs work as members of a team, instructing assistants while also taking instruction from directors and producers. Those making a film with a small budget may be required to oversee many different aspects of the production.

Filming challenges, such as how to shoot effectively underwater, in the dark, or in public areas, are a normal part of the job. DPs need patience in setting up cameras and preparing the lighting, as well as in dealing with the variety of professionals with whom they work.

OUTLOOK

The DOL predicts that employment for camera operators in the motion picture and video industries will grow about as fast as the the average for all careers through 2018. However, competition for work will be fierce because so many people are attracted to this business. Nevertheless, those with the right connections, strong samples of their work, and some luck are likely to find opportunities.

DPs of the future will be working more closely with special effects houses, even on films other than science fiction, horror, and other genres typically associated with special effects. Digital technology is used to create crowd scenes, underwater images, and other effects more efficiently and economically. DPs will have to approach a film with an understanding of which shots can be produced digitally and which will require traditional methods of filmmaking. DPs will also need to become familiar with the technology and techniques that are used to make 3D films—which have become very popular in Hollywood.

There will be more employment opportunities for those willing to work outside of the film industry at, for example, advertising agencies and TV broadcasting companies. The DOL anticipates that other types of programming, such as Internet broadcasts of music videos, sports, and other shows, will provide job openings in this field.

FOR MORE INFORMATION

For information about colleges with film and television programs of study, and to read interviews with filmmakers, visit the AFI Web site.
American Film Institute (AFI)
2021 North Western Avenue
Los Angeles, CA 90027-1657
Tel: 323-856-7600
E-mail: information@afi.com
http://www.afi.com

The ASC Web site has articles from American Cinematographer *magazine, industry news, and a tips and tricks for cinematographers section.*
American Society of Cinematographers (ASC)
PO Box 2230
Hollywood, CA 90078-2230
Tel: 800-448-0145
http://www.theasc.com

For information on union membership, contact
International Cinematographers Guild (IATSE Local 600)
National Office/Western Region
7755 Sunset Boulevard
Hollywood, CA 90046-3911
Tel: 323-876-0160
http://www.cameraguild.com

To read about film programs at several schools, visit the following Web sites:
New York Film Academy
http://www.nyfa.com

New York University
http://filmtv.tisch.nyu.edu/page/home

School of Visual Arts
http://schoolofvisualarts.edu

University of Southern California
http://cinema.usc.edu

Costume Designers

OVERVIEW

Costume designers plan, create, and maintain clothing and accessories for all characters in film, television, stage, dance, or opera productions. Designers custom fit each character, and either create a new garment or alter an existing costume.

HISTORY

Costume designers have worked in the motion picture industry ever since the first movies were made. But it was not until the 1920s that movie studios began establishing costume departments and costume designers began to receive film credits.

In 1948, the Academy of Motion Picture Arts and Sciences established the category for Best Costume Design, further spotlighting the importance of costume design in the movies. In 1953, the Costume Designers Guild was founded to represent the professional interests of costume designers.

Since the 1960s, new materials, such as plastics and adhesives, have greatly increased the costume designer's range. Today, their work is prominent in not only films, but also plays, musicals, dance performances, music videos, and television programs.

THE JOB

Costume designers generally work as freelancers. After they have been contracted to provide the costumes for a production, they read the script to learn about the theme, location, time period, character types, dialogue, and action. They meet with the director, production designer, and art director to discuss their feelings on the plot, characters, period and style, time frame for the production, and budget.

For a film, designers plan a rough costume plot, which is a list of costume changes by scene for each character. They thoroughly research the history and setting in which the movie is set. They plan a preliminary color scheme and sketch the costumes, including details such as gloves, footwear, hose, purses, jewelry, canes, fans,

Bob Ringwood, costume designer for Tim Burton's *Batman*, studies sketches. *(David Gamble, TopFoto/The Image Works)*

bouquets, and other props. The costume designer or an assistant collects swatches of fabrics and samples of various accessories.

After completing the research, final color sketches are painted or drawn and mounted for presentation. Costume designers may also use computer design programs to create the designs. Once the director approves the designs, the costume designer solicits bids from contractors, creates or rents costumes, and shops for fabrics and accessories. Measurements of all actors are taken. Designers work closely with drapers, sewers, hairstylists, and makeup artists in the costume shop. They supervise fittings and attend all dress rehearsals to make final adjustments and repairs.

Aside from working with actors, costume designers may also design and create costumes for performers such as figure skaters, ballroom dance competitors, circus members, theme park characters, rock artists, and others who routinely wear costumes as part of a show.

REQUIREMENTS

High School

Costume designers need at least a high school education. It is helpful to take classes in art, family and consumer science, and theater and to participate in drama clubs or community theater. English, literature, and history classes will help you learn how to analyze a play and research the clothing and manner of various historical periods. Marketing and business-related classes will also be helpful, as most costume designers work as freelancers. Familiarity with computers is useful, as many designers work with computer-aided design programs.

While in high school, consider starting a portfolio of design sketches. Practicing in a sketchbook is a great way to get ideas and designs out on paper and organized for future reference. You can also get design ideas through others; watch theater, television, or movie productions and take note of the characters' dress. Sketch them on your own for practice. Looking through fashion magazines can also give you ideas to sketch.

Postsecondary Training

A college degree is not a requirement, but in this highly competitive field, it provides a sizable advantage. Most costume designers today have a bachelor's degree. Many art schools, especially in New York and Los Angeles, have programs in costume design at both the bachelor's and master's degree level. A liberal arts school with a strong theater program is also a good choice. Additionally, some costume designers learn their skills through an apprenticeship.

Other Requirements

Costume designers need sewing, draping, and patterning skills, as well as training in basic design techniques and figure drawing. Aside from being artistic, designers must have good people skills because many compromises and agreements must be made between the designer and the film's director and/or production designer.

EXPLORING

If you are interested in costume design, consider joining a theater organization, such as a school drama club or a community theater. School dance troupes or film classes also may offer opportunities to explore costume design.

The Costume Designer's Handbook: A Complete Guide for Amateur and Professional Costume Designers, by Rosemary Ingham and Liz Covey (Portsmouth, N.H.: Heinemann Drama, 1992), is an invaluable resource for beginning or experienced costume designers. Other useful titles include *Costume Design 101: The Business and Art of Creating Costumes for Film and Television,* 2d edition, by Richard La Motte (Studio City, Calif.: Michael Wiese Books, 2010) and *Costuming for Film: The Art and the Craft,* by Holly Cole and Kristin Burke (Los Angeles: Silman-James Press, 2005).

You can practice designing on your own, by drawing original sketches or copying designs from television, films, or the stage. Practice sewing and altering costumes from sketches for yourself, friends and family.

EMPLOYERS

Costume designers are employed by production companies that produce works for stage, television, and film. Most employers are located in New York and Los Angeles, although most metropolitan areas have community theater and film production companies that hire designers.

STARTING OUT

Most high schools and colleges have drama clubs and dance groups that need costumes designed and made. Community theaters, too, may offer opportunities to assist in costume production. Regional theaters hire several hundred costume technicians each year for seasons that vary from 28 to 50 weeks.

Many beginning designers enter the field by becoming an assistant to a designer. Many established designers welcome newcomers and can be generous mentors. Some beginning workers start out in costume shops, which usually requires membership in a union. However, nonunion workers may be allowed to work for short-term projects. Some designers begin as *shoppers,* who swatch fabrics, compare prices, and buy yardage, trim, and accessories. Shoppers learn where to find the best materials at reasonable prices and often establish valuable contacts in the field. Other starting positions include milliner's assistant, craft assistant, or assistant to the draper.

Schools with bachelor's and master's programs in costume design may offer internships that can lead to jobs after graduation. Another method of entering costume design is to contact production companies directly and send your resume to the organization's hiring manager.

Before you become a costume designer, you may want to work as a freelance design assistant for a few years to gain helpful experience, a reputation, contacts, and an impressive portfolio.

ADVANCEMENT

Beginning designers must show they are willing to do a variety of tasks. By working hard and being flexible regarding work duties, they can gain a good reputation and be assigned more demanding tasks. Eventually, costume designers with experience and talent can work on larger productions. Some may even start their own freelance businesses.

EARNINGS

Earnings vary greatly for costume designers depending on factors such as how many outfits the designer completes, type of employer, how long they are employed during the year, and the amount of their experience. Although the U.S. Department of Labor (DOL) does not provide salary figures for costume designers, it does report statistics for the related occupational group of fashion designers. Those who worked in the motion picture and video industries earned $92,850 in 2009. Salaries for all fashion designers ranged from less than $32,320 to $130,900 or more.

For feature films and television, costume designers earn daily rates for an eight-hour day or a weekly rate for an unlimited number of hours. Designers sometimes earn royalties on their designs. Union costume designers working on major film or television productions earned union minimums of $2,888 for five days of work in 2010, according to the United Scenic Artists union.

Most costume designers work freelance and are paid per costume or film or production. Many costume designers must take second part-time or full-time jobs to supplement their income from costume design.

Salaried costume designers receive benefits such as health insurance and paid sick leave. Freelancers are responsible for their own health insurance, life insurance, and pension plans. They do not receive holiday, sick, or vacation pay.

WORK ENVIRONMENT

Costume designers put in long hours at painstaking detail work. It is a demanding profession that requires flexible, artistic, and practical workers. The schedule can be erratic—a busy period followed by weeks of little or no work. Though costumes are often a crucial part of a production's success, designers usually get little recognition compared to the actors and director.

Designers meet a variety of interesting and gifted people. Every film, play, or concert is different and every production situation is unique, so there is rarely a steady routine. Costume designers must play many roles: artist, sewer, researcher, buyer, manager, and negotiator.

OUTLOOK

Little change in employment is expected for fashion designers (a category that includes costume designers) through 2018, according to the DOL.

It is hard to obtain a position as a costume designer in the movie industry because the field is so small. Nevertheless, opportunities for costume designers exist. As demand for more American films increases from abroad, there will be a need for talented costume designers. Positions will also become available as designers retire or leave the industry for other reasons. There are also opportunities for costume designers outside the film industry, including in the theater industry. Costume designers are able to work in an increasing number of locations as new theaters are founded throughout the United States. As a result, however, designers must be willing to relocate. As more cable television networks create original programming, demand for costume design in this area should also increase.

FOR MORE INFORMATION

This union represents costume designers in film and television. For information on the industry and to view costume sketches, visit its Web site.

Costume Designers Guild
11969 Ventura Boulevard, 1st Floor
Studio City, CA 91604-2630
Tel: 818-752-2400
E-mail: cdgia@costumedesignersguild.com
http://www.costumedesignersguild.com

For information on costume design, contact

Costume Society of America
390 Amwell Road, Suite 402
Hillsborough, NJ 08844-1247
Tel: 800-272-9447
E-mail: national.office@costumesocietyamerica.com
http://www.costumesocietyamerica.com

For industry information, contact

National Costumers Association
121 North Bosart Avenue
Indianapolis, IN 46201-3729
Tel: 317-351-1940
E-mail: office@costumers.org
http://www.costumers.org

This union represents costume designers and other design professionals. For information on apprenticeship programs and other resources on the career, contact

United Scenic Artists Local USA 829
29 West 38th Street, 15th Floor
New York, NY 10018-5504
Tel: 212-581-0300
http://www.usa829.org

For information on opportunities in the performing arts and entertainment industry, contact

United States Institute for Theater Technology
315 South Crouse Avenue, Suite 200
Syracuse, NY 13210-1844
Tel: 800-938-7488
http://www.usitt.org

Film and Video Librarians

OVERVIEW

Librarians who oversee a collection of films and videos housed within a library, school, or business are called *film and video librarians,* or *media librarians.* They are in charge of researching, reviewing, purchasing, cataloging, and archiving the films and videos in all forms. The scope of the collection is dependent upon the type of institution or business in which they are employed.

Film and video librarians may also plan special viewing events or film discussion groups, or give class lectures. They take into account industry reviews and popular trends, as well as the input of the library director, teachers, students, and library patrons, when making new acquisitions. Many times they also maintain and provide instruction on the use of audiovisual equipment.

HISTORY

Although the career of film and video librarian has grown in popularity over the last several decades due to technological innovations and the growth of the motion picture, television, and educational media industries, this career actually began more than a century ago, according to the article "The History of Media Librarianship: A Chronology," by Amy Loucks-DiMatteo. In 1894, the Library of Congress housed the first paper or contact prints of motion pictures, and film librarians were needed to manage this collection. By approximately 1910, the Bell & Howell Film Company had assembled a film library of more than 1,200 silent and sound motion

QUICK FACTS

School Subjects
Computer science
English

Personal Skills
Helping/teaching
Leadership/management

Work Environment
Primarily indoors
Primarily one location

Minimum Education Level
Master's degree

Salary Range
$33,480 to $53,710 to
$82,450+

Certification or Licensing
Required by certain states

Outlook
About as fast as the average

DOT
100

GOE
12.03.04

NOC
5111

O*NET-SOC
25–4021.00

pictures. And by 1924, the American Library Association (ALA) recognized the growing importance of audiovisual libraries by creating a Visual Methods Committee to provide support to library professionals in this subfield.

The audiovisual library field grew in popularity over the next four decades. Major developments included the establishment of the first library audiovisual course at Peabody College in 1935; the publication of the book *Audiovisual School Library Service* (by Margaret Rufsvold), which offered instruction on how to establish an instructional materials center, in 1949; and the merging of many audiovisual libraries and traditional libraries into cohesive units in the 1950s and 1960s.

The introduction of home video in the 1970s created strong demand for librarians who specialized in audiovisual materials. Today, opportunities continue to be good for film and video librarians as a result of technological advancements and the increasing popularity of film and video as methods of entertainment and education.

THE JOB

Libraries are no longer limited to traditional collections of books and periodicals; they now include all forms of media, including

Movie Industry Facts

- The first Academy Awards were held on May 16, 1929.
- Academy Awards, often known as Oscars, are made of gold-plated britannium, a metal alloy. Each award is 13 inches tall and weighs 8 pounds.
- In 2009, the largest film studios by market share were: 1. Warner Bros.; 2. Paramount; 2. Sony/Columbia; 4. 20th Century Fox; 5. Buena Vista; and 6. Universal.
- The average movie admission for a family of four was $28.72 in 2009.
- Approximately 2.4 million people are employed in the American motion picture industry.

Sources: Academy of Motion Picture Arts and Sciences, Motion Picture Association of America, U.S. Department of Labor

music, film, and video. Those in charge of a special department or collection of film and videos are called film and video librarians, or media librarians. Their duties are similar to that of reference librarians, except their expertise is in film and video in all formats. Film and video librarians work in all types of libraries: public, governmental, corporate or special, and schools.

Film and video librarians are responsible for maintaining their library's collection of film and video. They catalog the items into the library's database according to their title, subject matter, or by actors/actresses and director. To prepare each film or video for circulation, each must be put in a protective covering or case, labeled with the library's name and address, and given a barcode and check-out card. Film and video librarians also archive and preserve existing material. They may also be responsible for the purchase and maintenance of audiovisual equipment.

It is the film and video librarian's responsibility to ensure that the collection meets with the specific interests of the institution. For example, medical libraries would be interested in health care issues; the library of a women's studies department would be interested in biographies, history, and events regarding women, women's rights, and other related issues. Film and video librarians at public institutions have the harder task of building a collection that appeals to different tastes or needs. They have a working knowledge of many different subject areas, including biographies of famous people, historical events, health, theater and the arts, popular culture, anime, and children's interests. This knowledge is important because they have to acquire items covering a plethora of topics and genres.

Librarians rely on reference guides, reviews, and recommendations from distributors when making important decisions on new acquisitions. They also take into account their department's budget, the school's curriculum, the needs of the educators, and patrons' requests. They must negotiate with distributors regarding pricing and public performance rights.

Film and video librarians may also plan special media events revolving around a film presentation or video night at their facility. In this instance, they would be responsible for scheduling the event, deciding on a theme, and marketing it to the public. At times, they may be asked by the school's faculty to help search for films to accompany a particular lesson plan or assignment. Librarians employed by government agencies may help acquire videos for special educational or training programs, such as a "Say No to Drugs" campaign.

Film and video librarians also have managerial duties. They hire, train, schedule, and supervise department staff. Along with the library director, or advisory board, they review the needs, policies, and direction of the department. They write reviews on new materials, compile bibliographies, and, at times, give a lecture on a particular film or video. They also help students or library patrons find information, answer questions, or give instruction on the proper use of audiovisual equipment. Film and video librarians rely on conferences, continuing education classes, and discussions with their peers to keep abreast of new technology or industry changes.

REQUIREMENTS

High School
Take classes in English, history, science, foreign languages, art, computer science, and mathematics to prepare for this career. Classes that require you to write numerous research papers will give you good experience in writing and utilizing different library resources. Film and video librarians will often give class lectures or hold discussion groups. If you dread speaking in front of a small group, consider taking a speech class or join the debate team to hone your verbal communication skills.

You should also take film classes or perhaps join a photography club. Such activities will give you familiarity with films outside of the mainstream and experience with different equipment.

Postsecondary Training
The direction you take in college depends largely on your place of employment. Many librarians working in a school setting hold an education degree with a specialization in media or information studies. Most, if not all, librarians working in college, corporate, or public libraries have a master's degree in library science (M.L.S.) or a master's degree in information systems (M.I.S.). It is important to have earned an M.L.S. or M.I.S. from a program that is accredited by the ALA. Most programs last from one to two years, with some schools offering off-site study opportunities. Many film and video librarians have a bachelor's degree in liberal arts and/or extensive experience in film.

Certification or Licensing
Certification and licensing requirements vary by state, county, and local government. Contact the school board in the area in which you plan to work for more information. If you work in a public elementary or secondary school, you will often be required to earn

teacher's certification and a master's degree in education in addition to preparation as a librarian.

Other Requirements

Film and video librarians must, first and foremost, have a love of film and video, and be willing to continue to learn about new technology throughout their careers. They must also have strong organizational skills, an attentiveness to detail, and the ability to interact well with coworkers and library patrons.

EXPLORING

A part-time job at a local library or your school's media center is a great way to explore this career. As a student you will probably be assigned small clerical tasks such as staffing the circulation desk, or straightening the stacks, but with some experience you may be assigned duties with more responsibilities. You might be able to eventually work as a media center aide, who sets up and maintains audiovisual equipment.

What better way to nurture your love of movies than by working at your local video store? Not only will you have access to the newest releases, but you'll also gain familiarity with films in a variety of subject areas.

You may want to participate in online discussion groups to get a feel for the industry. The ALA sponsors the Video Round Table (http://www.ala.org/ala/mgrps/rts/vrt/aboutvrt/vrtwelcome.cfm), an organization that addresses the interests of those working with video collections, programs, and services in libraries. This service is available to all ALA members.

EMPLOYERS

Although film and video librarians can find work in public or school libraries, the demand for this specialty is greatest in special libraries or those found in larger academic institutions. Reference librarians who work in small neighborhood libraries, or in media centers hosted within a school, may have film and video duties incorporated into their job responsibilities. Large metropolitan libraries often will have a separate film department with multiple staff. Universities, associations, or the government will also have an extensive film collection to warrant employing a film and video librarian on a full- or part-time basis.

STARTING OUT

There are many ways to enter this field. Some teachers decide to become librarians after having a fulfilling career in education. Reference librarians with a strong interest in films may choose to specialize in film and video acquisitions. Employment as an assistant film and video librarian is a common starting point and a great way to learn about the job and gain work experience.

Visit association Web sites to investigate the educational and certification requirements of librarians, as they vary from state to state. The ALA offers a wealth of information on this subject, including a list of employment opportunities nationwide, available awards, as well as grant and scholarship information.

ADVANCEMENT

There are many advancement opportunities available to film and video librarians. Librarians who work in smaller facilities may transfer to larger libraries where opportunities for job promotions and advancement are greater. It is also possible to move from one type of library to another. A librarian at a large public library may be responsible for a vast collection of biographies, documentaries, and instructional videos covering many different topics. A film and video librarian working for a corporation or nonprofit would only collect items dealing with that organization's interests or goals.

With sufficient work experience and education, those interested in administration may work as head of a film and video department, or even as a library director.

EARNINGS

Salaries for film and video librarians depend on such factors as the location, size, and type of library, the amount of experience the librarian has, and the responsibilities of the position. According to the U.S. Department of Labor (DOL), librarians had median annual earnings of $53,710 in 2009. Ten percent earned less than $33,480, and 10 percent earned $82,450 or more. Librarians working in colleges and universities earned $59,430 in 2009, and those employed by local government earned $49,920. In the federal government, the average salary for all librarians was $79,550.

Most film and video librarians receive a standard benefits package that includes paid vacation time, holiday pay, compensated sick leave, various insurance plans, and retirement savings programs.

WORK ENVIRONMENT

Film and video librarians employed at schools or public institutions have busy, often varied days. They may be researching possible new additions to the current collection one day, and teaching library staff members how to search for titles using a new online catalog the next. Disruptions are common, as patrons and staff will often turn to the film and video librarian with questions regarding a new documentary, or where to find an old black-and-white classic. Librarians working at a small library may be responsible for all duties in the film and video department, from reviewing and purchasing, to cataloging and maintenance. Those employed at a larger institution may have more administrative duties such as hiring, training, and supervising departmental staff, as well as setting work schedules.

Film and video librarians working for a special library do not usually have much interaction with the public. Much of their work—such as reviewing new acquisitions, reading trade publications and catalogs, and corresponding with distributors—is done independently.

Film and video librarians usually work a typical 40-hour week, Monday through Friday, with some weekend or evening hours as required. Some film and video librarians work part time. Those employed in an academic setting follow the school's schedule of summer and holiday breaks. Librarians often suffer from eyestrain due to long hours in front of the computer or reading print materials. Stress is another complication of this job. Film and video librarians often have to deal with multiple projects and deadlines.

OUTLOOK

The DOL predicts that employment for librarians will grow about as fast as the average for all careers through 2018. Opportunities should also be good for film and video librarians as more and more films and videos are released to educate and entertain the public. As with most careers, film and video librarians with advanced degrees and knowledge of the latest technology will have the best employment prospects.

FOR MORE INFORMATION

For a list of accredited schools and information on careers, scholarships and grants, and membership, contact

American Library Association
50 East Huron Street
Chicago, IL 60611-2729
Tel: 800-545-2433
http://www.ala.org

To learn more about information science careers, contact
American Society for Information Science and Technology
1320 Fenwick Lane, Suite 510
Silver Spring, MD 20910-3560
Tel: 301-495-0900
E-mail: asis@asis.org
http://www.asis.org

The association is a membership organization for media technology centers.
National Association of Media and Technology Centers
PO Box 9844
Cedar Rapids, IA 52409-9844
Tel: 319-654-0608
http://www.namtc.org

For information on working in a specialized library, contact
Special Libraries Association
331 South Patrick Street
Alexandria, VA 22314-3501
Tel: 703-647-4900
http://www.sla.org

For information on librarianship in Canada, contact
Canadian Library Association
1150 Morrison Drive, Suite 400
Ottawa, ON K2H 8S9 Canada
Tel: 613-232-9625
E-mail: info@cla.ca
http://www.cla.ca

Film Directors

OVERVIEW

"Lights! Camera! Action!" aptly summarizes the major responsibilities of the *film director*. In ultimate control of the decisions that shape a film production, the director is an artist who coordinates the elements of a film and is responsible for its overall style and quality.

Directors are well known for their part in guiding actors, but they are involved in much more—casting, costuming, cinematography, editing, and sound recording. Directors must have insight into the many tasks that go into the creation of a film, and they must have a broad vision of how each part will contribute to the big picture. Approximately 23,500 directors and producers are employed in the motion picture and video industries in the United States.

HISTORY

The playwrights and actors of ancient Greece were tellers of tales, striving to impress and influence audiences with their dramatic interpretations of stories. That tradition continues today on stages and film screens throughout the world.

From the days of the Greek theater until sometime in the 19th century, actors directed themselves. Although modern film directors can find their roots in the theater, it was not until the mid-1880s that the director became someone other than a member of the acting cast. It had been common practice for one of the actors involved in a production to be responsible not only for his or her own performance but also for conducting rehearsals and coordinating the tasks involved in putting on a play. Usually the most experienced and respected troupe member would guide the other actors, providing advice on speech, movement, and interaction.

A British actress and opera singer named Madame Vestris is considered to have been the first professional director. In the 1830s Vestris leased a theater in London and staged productions in which she herself did not perform. She displayed a new, creative approach to directing, making bold decisions about changing the traditional dress code for actors and allowing them to express their own interpretations of their roles. Vestris coordinated rehearsals, advised on lighting and sound effects, and chose nontraditional set decorations; she introduced props, such as actual windows and doors, that were more realistic than the usual painted panoramas.

By the turn of the century, theater directors such as David Belasco and Konstantin Stanislavsky had influenced the way in which performances were given, provoking actors and actresses to strive to identify with the characters they revealed so that audiences would be passionately and genuinely affected. By the early 1900s, Stanislavsky's method of directing performers had made an overwhelming mark on drama. His method (now often referred to as "the Method"), as well as his famous criticism, "I do not believe you," continues to influence performers to this day.

At this same time, the motion picture industry was coming into being. European filmmakers such as Leon Gaumont and New Yorker Edwin S. Porter were directing, filming, and producing short pictures. The industry's first professional female director was Alice Guy, who worked with Gaumont in the early years of the 20th century. The technical sophistication offered by today's professionals was not part of the early directors' repertoire. They merely filmed narratives without moving their camera. Soon directors began to experiment, moving the camera to shoot various angles and establishing a variety of editing techniques.

By 1915, there were close to 20,000 movie theaters in the United States; by the early 1920s, 40 million people were going to Hollywood-produced and -directed silent movies every week. Successful actors such as Charlie Chaplin and Buster Keaton began directing their own films, and Frank Capra and Cecil B. De Mille were starting their long careers as professional directors.

With the emergence of "talking pictures" in the early 1930s, the director's role changed significantly. Sound in film provided opportunities for further directorial creativity. Unnecessary noise could not be tolerated on the set; directors had to be concerned with the voices of their performers and the potential sound effects that could be created. Directors could demand certain types of voices (e.g., a Southern drawl) and sound effects (e.g., the rat-a-tat-tat of submachine guns) to present accurate interpretations of scripts. And no longer was the visually funny slapstick humor enough to make viewers laugh. Much of the humor in sound comedies arose from the script and from the successful direction of professionals like Frank Capra and Ernst Lubitsch.

The U.S. film industry experienced crises and controversy during the next 50 years, including financial problems, conglomerations of studios, and the introduction of the ratings system. New genres and elements began to challenge directorial genius over the years: science fiction, adventure, film noir; graphic representation of violence and sex; and sensational and computer-enhanced special effects. By the 1970s, university film schools had been established and were sending out creative directors, such as Francis Ford Coppola, George Lucas, Martin Scorsese, and Steven Spielberg, to name a few.

The continued development of new technologies has had a remarkable effect on the film and television industries. Advances such as computer-generated animation, digital filming, digital sound, 3-D technology, and high-definition television have given directors more tools to work with and the ability to produce an increasing variety of looks, sounds, characters—worlds—in their finished films or shows. Additionally, directors are using technologies not only to shape what the audience sees but also to determine where the audience sees it. Computers and the Internet have played a major role in the growth of the motion picture industry, with films available online and through

Learn More About It

Lanier, Troy, and Clay Nichols. *Filmmaking for Teens: Pulling Off Your Shorts.* 2d ed. Studio City, Calif.: Michael Wiese Productions, 2010.

Lowenstein, Stephen. (ed.) *My First Movie: Twenty Celebrated Directors Talk About Their First Film.* New York: Penguin Books, 2002.

Richards, Andrea. *Girl Director: A How-To Guide for the First-Time, Flat-Broke Film and Video Maker.* Berkeley, Calif.: Ten Speed Press, 2005.

Schneider, Steven Jay. *501 Movie Directors: A Comprehensive Guide to the Greatest Filmmakers.* Hauppauge, N.Y.: Barron's Educational Series, 2007.

downloads that can be viewed on personal computers, televisions, smart phones, MP3 players, and other devices. Such new tools for creating films and new avenues for presentation promise continued growth in this creative field.

THE JOB

Film directors, also called *filmmakers,* are considered to bear ultimate responsibility for the tone and quality of the films they work on. They interpret the stories and narratives presented in scripts and coordinate the filming of their interpretations. Two common techniques that categorize directors' styles are montage and mise-en-scene. *Montage directors* are concerned primarily with using editing techniques to produce desired results; they consider it important to focus on how individual shots will work when pieced together with others. Consider Alfred Hitchcock, who directed the production of one scene in *Psycho,* for example, by filming discrete shots in a bathroom and then editing in dialogue, sound effects, and music to create tremendous suspense. *Mise-en-scene directors* are more concerned with the pre-editing phase, focusing on the elements of angles, movement, and design one shot at a time, as Orson Welles did in many of his movies. Many directors combine elements of both techniques in their work.

Directors are involved in preproduction, production, and postproduction. They audition, select, and rehearse the acting crew; they work on matters regarding set designs, musical scores, and costumes; and they decide on details such as where scenes should be shot (on a soundstage, on location in a rainforest, etc.), what backgrounds might be needed, and how special and visual effects (such as computer-generated imagery, car crashes, or explosions) could be employed.

The director of a film often works with a *casting director,* who is in charge of auditioning performers. The casting director pays close attention to attributes of the performers such as physical appearance, quality of voice, and acting ability and experience, and then presents to the director a list of suitable candidates for each role.

One of the most important aspects of the film director's job is working with the performers. Directors have their own styles of extracting accurate emotion and performance from cast members, but they must be dedicated to this goal.

The director also works closely with the film's *production designer* to create set design concepts and choose shoot locations. The production designer meets with the filmmaker and producer to set budgets and schedules and then accordingly coordinates the construction of sets. Research is done on the period in which the film is to take place (for example, Elizabethan England, Pre-Columbian South America, or Los Angeles in the year 2500), and experts are consulted to help create appropriate architectural and environmental styles. The production designer also is often involved in design ideas for costumes, makeup and hairstyles, photographic effects, and other elements of the film's production. Production designers are assisted in this work by *art director*s. Low-budget films may just have an art director who handles the tasks of production designers.

The *director of photography,* or *cinematographer,* is responsible for organizing and implementing the actual camera work. Together with the filmmaker, he or she interprets scenes and decides on appropriate camera motion to achieve desired results. The director of photography determines the amounts of natural and artificial lighting required for each shoot and such technical factors as the type of film to be used, camera angles and distance, depth of field, and focus.

Motion pictures are usually filmed out of sequence, meaning that the ending might be shot first and scenes from the middle of the story might not be filmed until the end of production. Directors are responsible for scheduling each day's sequence of scenes; they coordinate filming so that scenes using the same set and performers will be filmed together. In addition to conferring with the production designer and the director of photography, filmmakers meet with technicians and crew members to advise on and approve final scenery, lighting, props, and other necessary equipment. They are also involved with final approval of costumes, choreography, and music.

After all the scenes have been shot, postproduction begins. The director works with *picture* and *sound edit*ors to organize the final film. The *film editor* shares the director's vision about the picture and assembles shots according to that overall idea, synchronizing film with voice and sound tracks produced by the sound editor and *music editor.*

While the director supervises all major aspects of film production, various assistants help throughout the process. In a less creative position than the filmmaker's, the *first assistant director* organizes various practical matters involved during the shooting of each scene. The *second assistant director* is a coordinator who works as a liaison among the production office, the first assistant director, and the performers. The *second unit director* coordinates sequences such as scenic inserts and action shots that do not involve the main acting crew.

Julie Delpy, writer/director of *2 Days in Paris,* reviews dailies on set. *(Samuel Goldwyn Films/Topham/The Image Works)*

Directors of computer-generated animation manage animators and artists on a daily basis, checking that their work meets design and thematic standards. They also work with production designers, art directors, and other production staff to make sure the project is manageable and meeting scheduling demands. Directors of computer-generated animation are knowledgeable about different software programs such as 3D Package and Maya.

REQUIREMENTS

High School

At the very least, a high school diploma, while not technically required if you wish to become a director, will still probably be indispensable to you in terms of the background and education it signifies. As is true of all artists, especially those in a medium as widely disseminated as film, you will need to have rich and varied experience in order to create works that are intelligently crafted and speak to people of many different backgrounds. In high school, courses in English, art, theater, and history will give you a good foundation. Further, a high school diploma will be necessary if you decide to go on to film school. Be active in school and community drama productions, whether as performer, set designer, or cue-card holder.

Postsecondary Training

In college and afterward, take film classes and volunteer to work on other students' films. Dedication, talent, and experience have always been indispensable to a director. No doubt it is beneficial to become aware of one's passion for film as early as possible. Woody Allen, for example, recognized early in his life the importance motion pictures held for him, but he worked as a magician, jazz clarinet player, joke writer, and stand-up comic before ever directing films. Allen took few film courses in his life.

On the other hand, many successful directors such as Francis Ford Coppola and Martha Coolidge have taken the formal film school route. There are more than 500 film studies programs offered by schools of higher education throughout the United States, including those considered to be the five most reputable: those of the American Film Institute in Los Angeles, Columbia University in New York City, New York University, the University of California

And the Oscar Goes To . . .

The following is a list of recent winners of the coveted Oscar for Best Director:

2010: Tom Hooper for *The King's Speech*
2009: Kathryn Bigelow for *The Hurt Locker*
2008: Danny Boyle for *Slumdog Millionaire*
2007: Joel Coen and Ethan Coen for *No Country for Old Men*
2006: Martin Scorsese for *The Departed*
2005: Ang Lee for *Brokeback Mountain*
2004: Clint Eastwood for *Million Dollar Baby*
2003: Peter Jackson for *Lord of the Rings: The Return of the King*
2002: Roman Polanski for *The Pianist*
2001: Ron Howard for *A Beautiful Mind*
2000: Steven Soderbergh for *Traffic*
1999: Sam Mendes for *American Beauty*
1998: Steven Spielberg for *Saving Private Ryan*
1997: James Cameron for *Titanic*
1996: Anthony Minghella for *The English Patient*
1995: Mel Gibson for *Braveheart*

For more information on Academy Award-winning directorial performances, visit http://awardsdatabase.oscars.org/ampas_awards/BasicSearchInput.jsp.

at Los Angeles, and the University of Southern California. These schools have accomplished film professionals on their faculties and provide a very visible stage for student talent, being located in the two film-business hot spots, California and New York. (The tuition for film programs offered elsewhere, however, tends to be much less expensive than at these schools.)

Film school offers overall formal training, providing an education in fundamental directing skills by working with student productions. Such education is rigorous, but in addition to teaching skills it provides aspiring directors with peer groups and a network of contacts with students, faculty, and guest speakers that can be of help after graduation. The debate continues on what is more influential in a directing career: film school or personal experience. Some say that it is possible for creative people to land directing jobs without having gone through a formal program. Competition is so pervasive in the industry that even film school graduates find jobs scarce.

Other Requirements

To be a successful film director, you must have good organizational skills, the ability to communicate with and manage others, a passion for filmmaking, and a creative vision that allows you to inspire others to help you create an entertaining and successful film.

EXPLORING

If you are an aspiring director, the most obvious opportunity for exploration lies in your own imagination. Being drawn to films and captivated by the process of how they are made is the beginning of the filmmaker's journey.

In high school and beyond, carefully study and pay attention to motion pictures. Watch them at every opportunity, both at the theater and at home. Two major trade publications to read are *Variety* (http://www.variety.com) and *Hollywood Reporter* (http://www.hollywoodreporter.com). The Directors Guild of America's official publications, *DGA Monthly and DGA Quarterly,* contain much information on the industry. Visit http://www.dga.org for more information.

During summers, many colleges, camps, and workshops offer programs for high school students interested in film work. For example, rising high school juniors and seniors and recent graduates can take courses in film and video for college credit via Columbia College Chicago's five-week High School Summer Institute. For

more information on this program, visit http://www.colum.edu/
Administrative_offices/Academic_Initiatives/APSI/index.php.

EMPLOYERS

Approximately 23,500 directors and producers are employed in the
motion picture and video industries in the United States. Film directors are usually employed on a freelance or contractual basis with
film studios (both major and independent). Directors can also find
work at television stations and cable networks, through advertising
agencies, with record companies, and through the creation of their
own independent film projects.

STARTING OUT

It is considered difficult to begin as a film director. With nontraditional steps to professional status, the occupation poses challenges
for those seeking employment. However, there is somewhat solid
advice for those who wish to direct motion pictures.

Many current directors began their careers in other film industry
professions, such as acting or writing. Consider Jodie Foster, who
appeared in 30 films and dozens of television productions before she
went on to direct her first motion picture at the age of 28. Obviously
it helps to grow up near the heart of "Tinseltown" and to have the
influence of one's family spurring you on. The support of family
and friends is often cited as an essential element in shaping the confidence you need to succeed in the industry.

As mentioned earlier, film school is a breeding ground for making
contacts in the industry. Often, contacts are the essential factor in
getting a job; many Hollywood insiders agree that it's not what you
know but whom you know that will get you in. Networking often
leads to good opportunities at various types of jobs in the industry.
Many professionals recommend that those who want to become
directors should go to Los Angeles or New York, find any industry-
related job, continue to take classes, and keep their eyes and ears
open for news of job openings, especially with those professionals
who are admired for their talent.

A program to be aware of is the Assistant Directors Training Program of the Directors Guild of America (its address is listed at the
end of this article). This program provides an excellent opportunity
to those without industry connections to work on film productions.
The program is based at two locations, New York City for the East
Coast program and Sherman Oaks, California, for the West Coast

program. Trainees receive hands-on experience, through placement with major studios or on television movies and series, and education, through mandatory seminars. The East Coast program requires trainees to complete at least 350 days of on-set production work; the West Coast program requires 400 days. While they are working, trainees are paid, beginning with a weekly salary of $651 in the East and $628 in the West. Once trainees have completed their program, they become freelance second assistant directors and can join the guild. Competition is extremely stiff for these positions.

Keep in mind that major studios in Hollywood are not the only place where directors work. Directors also work on documentaries, on television productions, and with various types of video presentations, from music to business. Honing skills at these types of jobs is beneficial for those still intent on directing for the big screen.

ADVANCEMENT

Advancement for film directors often comes in the form of recognition from their peers, professional film organizations, and the media. Directors who work on well-received movies receive awards as well as further job offers. Probably the most glamorized trophy is the Academy Award: the Oscar. Oscars are awarded in more than 20 categories, including one for best achievement in directing, and are given annually at a gala to recognize the outstanding accomplishments of those in the field.

Candidates for Oscars are usually judged by peers. Directors who have not worked on films popular enough to have made it in Hollywood should nevertheless seek recognition from reputable organizations. One such group is the National Endowment for the Arts, an independent agency of the U.S. government that supports and awards artists, including those who work in film. The endowment provides financial assistance in the form of fellowships and grants to those seen as contributing to the excellence of arts in the country.

EARNINGS

Directors' salaries vary greatly. Those just starting out in the industry might earn less than $10,000 a year, while big-name Hollywood directors can earn tens of millions of dollars annually. Most Hollywood film directors are members of the Directors Guild of America (DGA), and salaries (as well as hours of work and other employment conditions) are usually negotiated by this union. Generally, contracts provide for minimum weekly salaries. Keep in mind that because directors are freelancers, they may have no income for many weeks out of the year.

Although contracts usually provide only for the minimum rate of pay, most directors earn more, and they often negotiate extra conditions. Woody Allen, for example, takes the minimum salary required by the union for directing a film but also receives at least 10 percent of the film's gross receipts.

The U.S. Department of Labor (DOL) reports that the mean annual salary of directors who were employed in the motion picture and video industries was $108,580 in 2009. Salaries for all directors ranged from less than $30,560 to more than $111,250. Directors employed in cable broadcasting earned $86,680.

Directors working under DGA contracts also receive paid vacation days, lodging and meals while filming, and access to pension and health insurance plans.

WORK ENVIRONMENT

The work of the director is considered glamorous and prestigious, and of course directors have been known to become quite famous. But directors work under great stress, meeting deadlines, staying within budgets, and resolving problems among staff. "Nine-to-five" definitely does not describe a day in the life of a director; 16-hour days (and more) are not uncommon. Because directors are ultimately responsible for so much, schedules often dictate that they become immersed in their work around the clock, from preproduction to final cut. Nonetheless, those able to make it in the industry find their work to be extremely enjoyable and satisfying.

OUTLOOK

Employment for directors who work in the motion picture and video industries is expected to grow about as fast as the average for all occupations through 2018, according to the DOL. This forecast is based on the increasing global demand for films and television programming made in the United States, continuing U.S. demand for home video and DVD rentals, and the development of other delivery methods for films, such as the Internet and smart phones and other portable electronic devices. However, competition is extreme and turnover is high. Most positions in the motion picture industry are held on a freelance basis. As is the case with most film industry workers, directors are usually hired to work on one film at a time. After a film is completed, new contacts must be made for further assignments.

Television offers directors a wider variety of employment opportunities such as directing sitcoms, made-for-television movies, newscasts, commercials, even music videos. The number of cable television networks is growing, and directors are needed to help create original programming to fill this void. Half of all television directors work as freelancers. This number is predicted to rise as more cable networks and production companies attempt to cut costs by hiring directors on a project-to-project basis.

FOR MORE INFORMATION

For information on the AFI Conservatory, AFI workshops, AFI awards, and other film and television news, visit the AFI Web site or contact
American Film Institute (AFI)
2021 North Western Avenue
Los Angeles, CA 90027-1657
Tel: 323-856-7600
E-mail: information@afi.com
http://www.afi.com

Visit the DGA Web site for information on publications and links to film schools and film festivals.
Directors Guild of America (DGA)
7920 Sunset Boulevard
Los Angeles, CA 90046-3304
Tel: 310-289-2000
http://www.dga.org

For more information about the DGA Assistant Directors Training Program, visit these Web sites
East Coast Program
http://www.dgatrainingprogram.org

West Coast Program
http://www.trainingplan.org

This is the trade association of the American film industry and home video and television industries. It operates the voluntary movie ratings system in cooperation with the National Association of Theatre Owners.

Motion Picture Association of America
1600 Eye Street, NW
Washington, DC 20006-4010
Tel: 202-293-1966
http://www.mpaa.org

Women in Film's mission is to "empower, promote, and mentor women in the entertainment and media industries." Visit its Web site to learn about membership, internships, competitions, and financial aid for college students.

Women in Film
6100 Wilshire Boulevard, Suite 710
Los Angeles, CA 90048-5107
Tel: 323-935-2211
E-mail: info@wif.org
http://www.wif.org

Film Editors

OVERVIEW

Film editors perform an essential role in the motion picture industry. They take an unedited draft of film, videotape, or digital video and use specialized equipment to improve the draft until it is ready for viewing. It is the responsibility of the film editor to create the most effective product possible. Approximately 11,800 editors are employed in the motion picture and video industries in the United States.

HISTORY

In the early days of the industry, editing was sometimes done by directors, studio technicians, or other film staffers. Now every film (as well as television shows and video, including the most brief television advertisement) has an editor who is responsible for the continuity and clarity of the project.

The motion picture industry has experienced substantial growth in the United States. As more people have access to cable television and the Internet, MP3 players, and other technology, the industry has continued to grow. The effect of this growth is a steady demand for the essential skills that film editors provide. With recent innovations in computer technology, much of the work that these editors perform is accomplished using sophisticated software programs. All of these factors have enabled many film editors to find steady work as salaried employees of film production companies and as independent contractors who provide their services on a per-job basis.

And the Oscar Goes To . . .

The following is a list of some of the film editors who have won Oscars for their work:

2010: Angus Wall and Kirk Baxter for *The Social Network*
2009: Bob Murawski and Chris Innis for *The Hurt Locker*
2008: Chris Dickens for *Slumdog Millionaire*
2007: Christopher Rouse for *The Bourne Ultimatum*
2006: Thelma Schoonmaker for *The Departed*
2005: Hughes Winborne for *Crash*
2004: Thelma Schoonmaker for *The Aviator*
2003: Jamie Selkirk for *Lord of the Rings: The Return of the King*
2002: Martin Walsh for *Chicago*
2001: Pietro Scalia for *Black Hawk Down*
2000: Stephen Mirrione for *Traffic*
1999: Zach Staenberg for *The Matrix*
1998: Michael Kahn for *Saving Private Ryan*
1997: Conrad Buff, James Cameron, and Richard A. Harris for *Titanic*
1996: Walter Murch for *The English Patient*
1995: Mike Hill and Dan Hanley for *Apollo 13*

For more information on Academy Award-winning editors, visit http://awardsdatabase.oscars.org/ampas_awards/BasicSearchInput .jsp.

THE JOB

Film editors work closely with producers and directors throughout an entire project. These editors assist in the earliest phase, called preproduction, and during the production phase, when actual filming occurs. However, their skills are in the greatest demand during postproduction, when primary filming is completed.

During preproduction, editors meet with producers to learn about the objectives of the film. If the project is a feature-length motion picture, for example, the editor must understand the storyline. The producer may explain the larger scope of the project so that the editor knows the best way to approach the work when it is time to edit the film. In consultation with the director, editors may discuss the best way to present the screenplay or script. They may discuss different settings, scenes, or camera angles even before filming begins. With this kind of preparation, film editors are ready to practice their craft as soon as the production phase is complete.

Feature-length films take a considerable amount of time to edit. Some editors may spend months on one project, while others may work on several shorter projects simultaneously.

Editors are usually the final decision makers when it comes to choosing which segments will stay in as they are, which segments will be cut, or which may need to be redone. Editors look at the quality of the segment, its dramatic value, and its relationship to other segments. They then arrange the segments in an order that creates the most effective finished product. Some editors have specialized duties. *Sound editors* work on the soundtracks of television programs or motion pictures. They often keep libraries of sounds that they reuse for various projects. These include natural sounds, such as thunder or raindrops, animal noises, motor sounds, or musical interludes. Some sound editors specialize in music and may have training in music theory or performance. Others work with sound effects. They may use unusual objects, machines, or computer-generated noisemakers to create a desired sound for a film or TV show.

The digital revolution has greatly affected the editing process. Many editors now use computer programs such as AVID, Lightworks,

Editors must be skilled at using film editing software programs to edit footage. *(Bob Finlayson, Newspix/News Ltd.)*

or Final Cut Pro to do their jobs. They also work much more closely with special and visual effects houses in putting together projects. When working on projects that have a large number of special and visual effects, film editors edit scenes with an eye towards the special and visual effects that will be added. Digital editing technology may allow some prospective editors more direct routes into the industry, but the majority of editors will have to follow traditional routes, obtaining years of hands-on experience to advance in their career.

REQUIREMENTS

High School

Broadcast journalism and other media and communications courses may provide you with practical experience in video editing. Because film editing requires creativity along with technical skills, you should take English, speech, theater, and other courses that will allow you to develop writing skills. Art and photography classes will involve you with visual media. If you're lucky enough to attend a high school that offers classes in either film history or film production, be sure to take those courses. The American Film Institute's Web site (http://www.afi.com/education/Conservatory) offers listings of high schools with film courses and other resources for teachers and students. Finally, don't forget to take computer classes. Film editors constantly makes use of new technology, and you should become familiar and comfortable with computers as soon as possible.

Postsecondary Training

Some studios require film editors to have a bachelor's degree. Many film schools offer classes or degrees in film editing. Some schools, such as the American Film Institute, offer graduate degrees in film editing.

Many editors learn much of their work on the job as an assistant or apprentice at larger studios that offer these positions. During an apprenticeship, the apprentice has the opportunity to see the work of the editor up close. The editor may eventually assign some of his or her minor duties to the apprentice, while still making the larger decisions. After a few years the apprentice may be promoted to editor or may apply for a position as a film editor at other studios. Training in film and video editing is also available in the military.

Other Requirements

You should be able to work cooperatively with other creative people when editing a project. You should remain open to suggestions and guidance, while also maintaining your confidence and hold your own opinion in the presence of other professionals. A successful editor has an understanding of the history of film and a feel for the narrative form in general. Computer skills are also important and will help you to learn new technology in the field. You may be required to join a union to do this work, depending on the studio. You should have a good visual understanding, and you need to be able to tell a story and be aware of everything that is going on in a frame.

EXPLORING

Many high schools have film clubs, and some have cable television or Internet-based stations affiliated with the school district. Often school-run television channels give students the opportunity to create and edit short programs. Check out what's available at your school.

One of the best ways to prepare for a career as a film editor is to read widely. By reading literature, you will develop your understanding of the different ways in which stories can be presented. You can also read books about work as a film editor. Here are two suggestions: *Film Editing: Great Cuts Every Filmmaker and Movie Lover Must Know,* by Gael Chandler (Studio City, Calif.: Michael Wiese Books, 2009) and *The Technique of Film and Video Editing: History, Theory, and Practice,* 4th ed., by Ken Dancyger (St. Louis, Mo.: Focal Press, 2006).

You should be familiar with many different kinds of film projects, including documentaries, short films, and feature films, as well as nonfilm-based offerings such as TV shows, music videos, and commercials. See as many different projects as you can and study them, paying close attention to the decisions the editors made in piecing together the scenes. Additionally, many DVDs now have special features such as interviews with film directors, producers, and editors. By viewing these, you can get a good idea about the decisions that are made during the creation of a film.

Large film companies occasionally have volunteers or student interns. Most people in the industry start out doing minor tasks helping with production. These production assistants get the opportunity to see all of the professionals at work. By working closely with an editor, a production assistant can learn film operations as well as specific editing techniques.

EMPLOYERS

There are approximately 11,800 editors employed in the motion picture and video industries in the United States. Motion picture studios are the main employers of film editors. Editors may develop ongoing working relationships with directors or producers who hire them from one project to another. Many editors who have worked for a studio or postproduction company for several years often become independent contractors. These editors offer their services on a per-job basis to producers of films, negotiate their own fees, and typically purchase or lease their own editing equipment. Other editors are employed by television news stations, television production companies, music video producers, and production companies that produce commercials and other projects that require editors.

STARTING OUT

Because of the glamour associated with film work, this is a popular field that can be very difficult to break into. With a minimum of a high school diploma or a degree from a two-year college, you can apply for entry-level jobs in many film studios, but these jobs will not be editing positions. Most studios will not consider people for film editor positions without a bachelor's degree or several years of on-the-job experience.

One way to get on-the-job experience is to complete an apprenticeship in editing. However, in some cases, you won't be eligible for an apprenticeship unless you are a current employee of the studio. Therefore, start out by applying to as many film studios as possible and take an entry-level position, even if it is not in the editing department. Once you start work, let people know that you are interested in an editor apprenticeship so that you'll be considered the next time a position becomes available.

Those who have completed bachelor's or master's degrees have typically gained hands-on experience through school projects. Another benefit of going to school is that contacts that you make while in school, both through your school's career services office and alumni, can be a valuable resource when you look for your first job. Your school's career services office may also have listings of job openings. Some studio work is union regulated. Therefore you may also want to contact union locals to find out about job requirements and openings.

Professional associations also provide job assistance to their members. For example, American Cinema Editors allows its members to post their resumes at its Web site.

ADVANCEMENT

Once film editors have secured employment in their field, their advancement comes with further experience and greater recognition.

Some film editors develop good working relationships with directors or producers. These editors may be willing to leave the security of a studio job for the possibility of working one-on-one with the director or producer on a project. These opportunities often provide editors with the autonomy they may not get in their regular jobs. Some are willing to take a pay cut to work on a project they feel is important.

Some film editors choose to stay at their studios and advance through seniority to editing positions with higher salaries. They may be able to negotiate better benefits packages or to choose the projects they will work on. They may also choose which directors they wish to work with. In larger studios, editors may train and supervise staffs of less experienced or apprentice editors.

Some sound editors may wish to broaden their skills by working as general film editors. Some film editors may, on the other hand, choose to specialize in sound effects, music, animation, or some other editorial area. Some editors who work in film may move to television or may move from working on commercials or television series to movies.

EARNINGS

Film editors are not as highly paid as others working in their industry. They have less clout than directors or producers, but they have more authority in the production of a project than many other film professionals. According to the U.S. Department of Labor (DOL), mean annual earnings for film editors working in motion pictures and videos were $70,330 in 2009. The most experienced and sought-after film editors can command much higher salaries. Salaries for all editors ranged from less than $25,400 to $112,960 or more.

Benefits for full-time workers include vacation and sick time, health, and sometimes dental, insurance, and pension or 401(k) plans. Self-employed editors must provide their own benefits.

WORK ENVIRONMENT

Most of the work performed by editors is done in film studios or at postproduction companies. The working environment is often a small studio office cramped full of editing equipment. Working hours vary widely depending on the project. Many feature-length films are kept on tight production schedules. Editors may be required to work overtime, at night, or on weekends to finish the project by an assigned date. The work can be stressful, but it can also be satisfying and fun.

During filming, editors may be asked to be on hand at the filming location. Locations may be outdoors or in other cities, and travel is occasionally required. More often, however, the film editor works in the studio.

Disadvantages of the job involve the editor's low rank on the totem pole of film industry jobs. However, most editors feel that this is outweighed by the honor of working on exciting projects.

OUTLOOK

Employment for film editors will grow about as fast as the average for all occupations through 2018, according to the DOL. The growth of cable television, the increase in the number of independent film studios, and the emergence of the Internet, MP3 players, and other computer technologies as means to view movies will translate into greater demand for editors. This will also force the largest studios to offer more competitive salaries in order to attract the best film editors. Opportunities will also be available outside the film industry with television studios and broadcast stations.

FOR MORE INFORMATION

The ACE features career and education information for film editors on its Web site, along with information about internship opportunities and sample articles from CinemaEditor *magazine.*

American Cinema Editors (ACE)
100 Universal City Plaza
Verna Fields Building 2282, Room 190
Universal City, CA 91608-1002
Tel: 818-777-2900
http://www.ace-filmeditors.org

For information about the AFI Conservatory's master of fine arts in editing and to read interviews with professionals, visit the AFI Web site.

American Film Institute (AFI)
2021 North Western Avenue
Los Angeles, CA 90027-1657
Tel: 323-856-7600
E-mail: information@afi.com
http://www.afi.com

For information about union membership, contact
Motion Picture Editors Guild
7715 Sunset Boulevard, Suite 200
Hollywood, CA 90046-3912
Tel: 323-876-4770
E-mail: mail@editorsguild.com
https://www.editorsguild.com

For information on sound editing, contact
Motion Picture Sound Editors
10061 Riverside Drive
PMB Box 751
Toluca Lake, California 91602-2550
Tel: 818-506-7731
E-mail: mail@mpse.org
http://www.mpse.org

For information on career opportunities in the television industry,
visit the NATAS Web site.
National Academy of Television Arts and Sciences (NATAS)
1697 Broadway, Suite 1001
New York, NY 10019-5906
Tel: 212-586-8424
E-mail: hq@natasonline.com
http://www.emmyonline.org

Women in Film's mission is to "empower, promote, and mentor
women in the entertainment and media industries." Visit its Web
site to learn about membership, internships, competitions, and
financial aid for college students.
Women in Film
6100 Wilshire Boulevard, Suite 710
Los Angeles, CA 90048-5107
Tel: 323-935-2211
E-mail: info@wif.org
http://www.wif.org

Film Extras

OVERVIEW

Film extras, also known as *background performers,* have nonspeaking roles in films. They work in the background of film scenes, following the orders of directors and crew members. They may work in crowd scenes, or may simply be one of a few people among the principal performers.

HISTORY

Ever since the dawn of filmmaking more than 110 years ago, filmmakers have understood the importance of using extras to lend authenticity to a scene. Particularly in the silent era, visual effects were very important; people were employed to move about the makeshift sets of a film production to help viewers understand the size of the city portrayed, the number of people affected by the film's events, and other details. D. W. Griffith's *Intolerance,* made in 1916, is one of the earliest and most infamous examples of a big-budget production that relied a great deal on extravagant sets and huge crowd scenes. Extras were dressed in a variety of period costume and recreated epic battle scenes. In one sequence, extras storm the immense walls of ancient Babylon; in another, extras play factory workers shot down by police. Today, large crowd scenes are still used in big productions to provide scenes with greater power and scope. Though computer-generated images are increasingly used to fill out the crowd scenes of such films as *Elizabeth* and *Titanic,* many extras are still used. For *Titanic,* these extras were filmed in costume in a room, and added later to the deck of the digitally created ship.

QUICK FACTS

School Subjects
Speech
Theater/dance

Personal Skills
Artistic
Following instructions

Work Environment
Indoors and outdoors
Primarily multiple locations

Minimum Education Level
High school diploma

Salary Range
$500 to $5,000 to $15,000

Certification or Licensing
None available

Outlook
Faster than the average

DOT
159

GOE
01.05.01

NOC
N/A

O*NET-SOC
N/A

THE JOB

When you go to the movies, you probably do not pay close attention to the people in the background of all the scenes. Yet, if they were not there—if there were no lines at the bank, no crowds at the football game, no passengers on the airplane—you would certainly notice. Practically every filmmaker uses extras. Though these extras do not have lines, close-ups, or any real significance to the film's plot, they are important in establishing the world of the film.

Many people work as extras to gain professional experience, hoping to someday become *principal actors* (performers in featured roles), or to work in the film industry in some other capacity. Others, like John Sharpe, simply see extra work as an enjoyable way to supplement their incomes. "I work mostly with shows and movies that need high school and college-age-looking kids," Sharpe says. He has worked on the film *She's All That,* and his TV credits include *Buffy the Vampire Slayer* and *Party of Five.*

"It's easy to become an extra," he says. "Anyone can register at a nonunion extra casting agency. There are several of them in the Los Angeles area. When you have a day you can work, you call their recorded line and see if they need anyone of your description. If so, you call an agent in their office and they book you for it."

If selected, film extras are advised on what they need to bring to the set and when and where to report to work. For most films, extras are asked to wear their own clothes. For a film set in another time period, they may have to report to the wardrobe department for a costume fitting.

In some cases, a casting director for a film will be looking for specific types and talents. For example, if a scene features a baseball game, the director may need extras who can pitch, hit, and run. Or a period scene in a dance hall may call for extras who know certain traditional dances. These extras are called *special ability extras* and usually receive better daily pay than general extras. A *stand-in* may also be needed for a film shoot. A stand-in is an extra who takes the place of a principal actor when the crew prepares to film a scene, but who is not actually filmed. Stand-ins are positioned on the set for the cameras to focus the shot and set up lights.

Members of the Screen Actors Guild (SAG), the union for film actors and extras, generally receive better pay than nonunion extras. A film must have 30 SAG-registered extras on a given day before hiring nonunion extras.

When reporting for work, extras may be part of a rehearsal or may be thrust immediately into the filming of the scene. They are required

Movie extras are filmed in Rome's Old Ghetto for a film set during World War II. *(Plinio Lepri, AP Photo)*

to pay close attention to the director and cooperate with crew members. Extras may be asked to simply stand in the background, to have conversation with other extras, or to move freely about the set. They must keep track of what they are doing in each scene in order to help maintain continuity from scene to scene. Extras may have to repeat their actions, gestures, and expressions again and again until the filmmakers have the shot they need. Their scene may only take a few hours to complete or may take several days. Extras may be used for the background in only one scene or may be used in many scenes. In rare cases, an extra is plucked from a crowd scene and given a line to speak. In this case, the performer is considered a *day player.*

REQUIREMENTS

High School

Many children and high school students work as extras in films (as well as television shows). Though you won't need special training to become a film extra, you should at least obtain a high school diploma. Classes that may be helpful to you in your work as an extra include theater, dance, and speech.

Postsecondary Training

There is no postsecondary training required for film extras. Those who are interested in a career as an actor are strongly advised to complete at least a bachelor's degree program in theater or the dramatic arts.

Other Requirements

Union membership can be helpful in finding work and earning better pay, but it isn't required for you to work as an extra. Generally, performers apply for SAG membership after finding success in working as an extra for a time. See the end of the article for SAG's contact information to learn more.

Extras need to be punctual, attentive, and capable of following instructions closely. "You need to be responsible and dependable first and foremost," John Sharpe says.

Extras should also be patient, as they may spend much of their time waiting around, or doing the same things repeatedly.

EXPLORING

One of the best ways to explore the field is to actually work as a film extra. Nearly all states have at least one film commission that offers information about local productions and opportunities for actors and extras. Visit the Association of Film Commissioners International's Web site, http://www.afci.org, for information about more than 300 film commissions on six continents. Other ways to explore the work of film extras is to act in school drama productions; write, act in, and film your own movies; read books and visit Web sites about the film industry; and talk to film extras about the pros and cons of the field.

EMPLOYERS

Because of the nature of the work, extras don't have a regular employer, though they may work for some of the same filmmakers and TV productions. In addition to movies, extras are needed for television shows, commercials, music videos, and interactive games.

STARTING OUT

For regular work as a film extra, you will have more success living where the bulk of films are filmed, around Los Angeles or New York. Though some productions may place ads for extras in local newspapers or on the Internet, you will benefit the most by having an agent. There are agents who work exclusively with extras, as opposed to principal actors agents. Extras agents typically charge a registration fee (usually under $30) and a 5 to 10 percent commission. When selecting an agent, be very careful of scams; carefully read any contract and be wary of agents with large registration fees or those who claim to "guarantee" work. For information about reputable agents, you can check with your local film commission or local division of SAG.

ADVANCEMENT

Becoming a member of SAG ensures extras and other performers better pay. Union membership can also help to establish contacts and possibly locate more work. "If you plan to pursue acting, extra work is probably the best way into SAG," John Sharpe says. "Spending so much time on sets is a good way to learn about the industry and even to make connections."

By talking to other extras and crew members, beginning performers can learn more about the film industry and may make some valuable connections. Unfortunately, there are no guarantees for success in the film industry; even years of experience in the industry may eventually lead nowhere. However, extras may be able to use connections they've made through union membership and working on productions to get more major auditions for supporting or major roles on films and TV shows.

EARNINGS

It is very rare that someone is able to make a living solely from work as an extra. According to SAG, a majority of its nearly 120,000 members make less than $7,500 a year. SAG sets daily wage minimums for its members, which vary according to city and type of extra work. For example, in 2010, extras made at least $139 a day. If they had a part showing off a special ability or talent, they were paid $149 or more a day. Extras also earn more if they have to work in rain or smoke, or if they are required to wear body makeup, wigs, or a certain haircut for the part. If they supply their own props, such as pets, cars, golf clubs, or luggage, extras also are paid higher daily rates.

Any extra who is upgraded to a speaking part—even just one line of dialogue—is considered a day player and earns significantly more per day.

WORK ENVIRONMENT

The work of a film extra is unsteady, but many people enjoy the opportunity to see themselves on screen. Though the work is not terribly glamorous, extras do have the chance to see famous actors and filmmakers practice their craft. Extras can work indoors on a set or outdoors at a remote location. They work under heavy lights and may be required to do the same things over and over. There may also be a great deal of downtime as extras wait for cast and crew to prepare for a shot. "It's not rare to work a 12- to 14-hour day," John Sharpe says, "so you need to be flexible."

OUTLOOK

It is estimated that hundreds of thousands of people act every year. Because of the fierce competition, jobs in the film industry are hard to come by. Extras who live in Los Angeles or New York City and have an extras agent are likely more able to find work, but the low pay and the unsteady nature of the work usually prevent them from making a comfortable living as an extra.

The U.S. Department of Labor predicts that employment in the film industry will grow faster than the average for all industries through 2018. Though the competition for jobs is high, many individuals leave acting for a more stable and higher income. Because of the high turnover, opportunities for work are always available; performers with patience, confidence and stamina will stand a higher chance at success in the acting business.

FOR MORE INFORMATION

For information about membership, wages, and advice on filmmaking and acting, contact the following unions:

American Federation of Television & Radio Artists
260 Madison Avenue
New York, NY 10016-2401
Tel: 212-532-0800
http://www.aftra.org

International Alliance of Theatrical Stage Employees, Moving Picture Technicians, Artists and Allied Crafts of the United States and Canada
1430 Broadway, 20th Floor
New York, NY 10018-3348
Tel: 212-730-1770
http://www.iatse-intl.org

Screen Actors Guild
5757 Wilshire Boulevard, 7th Floor
Los Angeles, CA 90036-3600
Tel: 800-724-0767
E-mail: saginfo@sag.org
http://www.sag.org

Film Writers

QUICK FACTS

School Subjects
English
Journalism

Personal Skills
Communication/ideas
Helping/teaching

Work Environment
Primarily indoors
One location with some
  travel

Minimum Education Level
Bachelor's degree

Salary Range
$28,070 to $85,420 to
$105,710+

Certification or Licensing
None available

Outlook
About as fast as the average

DOT
131

GOE
01.02.01

NOC
5121

O*NET-SOC
27–3043.00

OVERVIEW

Film writers express, edit, promote, and interpret ideas and facts about films and the motion picture industry in written form for newspapers, magazines, books, Web sites, and radio and television broadcasts. (For information about writers who create scripts for films, see the article on Screenwriters.) There are approximately 151,700 salaried writers in the United States; however, only about 2,000 are film writers.

HISTORY

The famous inventor Thomas Edison produced a short movie called *The Sneeze* in 1894, using film for the first time instead of individual plates. Georges Melies introduced narrative films in 1899 in France, and in 1903 Edwin Porter filmed *The Great Train Robbery,* the first motion picture that told a story using modern filming techniques.

Motion pictures became increasingly popular in the early 1900s, with the advent of the movie house and silent film stars such as Charlie Chaplin and Rudolph Valentino. It was not until 1927, when *The Jazz Singer* with Al Jolson was produced, that talking movies began to be made.

As the film industry grew, so did the number of publications that began to cover this fast-growing and glamorous industry. Some, such as *Variety* (founded in 1905) and *Hollywood Reporter* (1930), are still reporting on the film industry today.

In addition to the print media, the broadcasting industry has contributed to the development of the professional film writer. Radio,

Useful Web Sites for Film Writers

FilmCritic.com
http://www.filmcritic.com

Film Festivals.com
http://www.filmfestivals.com

Internet Movie Database
http://www.imdb.com

Movie City News
http://www.moviecitynews.com

Roger Ebert.com
http://rogerebert.suntimes.com

Senses of Cinema
http://www.sensesofcinema.com

television, and the Internet are sources of information, education, and entertainment that provide employment for thousands of film writers.

THE JOB

Film writers write about the motion picture industry, its actors and other professionals, films, genres, companies, technologies, events, history, and any other topic that relates to the field. The nature of their work is as varied as the venues for which they write: newspapers, magazines, books, and Web sites and blogs. Some film writers also appear on television and radio talk shows and documentaries.

Film staff writers are employed by magazines and newspapers to write news stories, feature articles, and columns about the film industry. First they come up with an idea for an article from their own interests or are assigned a topic by an editor. The topic is of relevance to the particular publication; for example, a writer for an animation magazine may be assigned an article on the Academy Award for animation. A writer for a film history magazine may come up with the idea of interviewing one of the last living actors from a famous film such as *Casablanca*. A writer for a weekly entertainment section in a newspaper may be assigned to interview the lead actor in the latest science fiction blockbuster.

After writers receive their assignments, they begin gathering as much information as possible about the subject through library research, interviews, the Internet, observation, and other methods. They keep extensive notes from which they will draw material for their project. Once the material has been organized and arranged in logical sequence, writers prepare a written outline. The process of developing a piece of writing is exciting, although it can also involve detailed and solitary work. After researching an idea, a writer might discover that a different perspective or related topic would be more effective, entertaining, or marketable.

When working on assignment, writers usually submit their outlines to an editor or other company representative for approval. Then they write a first draft, trying to put the material into words that will have the desired effect on their audience. They often rewrite or polish sections of the material as they proceed, always searching for just the right way of imparting information or expressing an idea or opinion. A manuscript may be reviewed, corrected, and revised numerous times before a final copy is submitted. Even after that, an editor may request additional changes.

Film columnists or *commentators* analyze news and social issues as they relate to the motion picture industry. They write about events from the standpoint of their own experience or opinion.

Film critics review movies for print publications and television and radio stations. They tell readers and listeners why or why not, in their opinion, they should spend their money to see a movie. Film critics may also interview actors, directors, and other film professionals for print articles and broadcast interviews. Some film critics, such as Roger Ebert, become celebrities in their own right.

Writers can be employed either as in-house staff or as freelancers. Pay varies according to experience and the position, but freelancers must provide their own office space and equipment such as computers and fax machines. Freelancers also are responsible for keeping tax records, sending out invoices, negotiating contracts, and providing their own health insurance.

REQUIREMENTS

High School
While in high school, build a broad educational foundation by taking courses in English, literature, foreign languages, history, general science, social studies, computer science, and typing. The ability to type is almost a requisite for many positions in the journalism field, as is familiarity with computers. If you are interested in becoming a

film writer, you should watch as many films as possible, as well as read film-related publications.

Postsecondary Training

Competition for journalistic writing jobs almost always demands the background of a college education. Many employers prefer you have a broad liberal arts background or majors in English, literature, history, philosophy, or one of the social sciences. Other employers desire communications or journalism training in college. Occasionally a master's degree in a specialized writing field may be required. Many schools offer courses in journalism, and some of them offer courses or majors in newspaper and magazine writing, publication management, book publishing, and writing for the Internet. If you are interested in film writing, you might want to consider a major, or at least a minor, in a film-related area.

In addition to formal course work, most employers look for practical writing experience. If you have worked on high school or college newspapers, yearbooks, or literary magazines, you will make a better candidate, as well as if you have worked for small community newspapers or radio stations, even in an unpaid position. Many magazines, newspapers, and radio and television stations have summer internship programs that provide valuable training if you want to learn about the publishing and broadcasting businesses. Interns do many simple tasks, such as running errands and answering phones, but some may be asked to perform research, conduct interviews, or even write some minor pieces.

Other Requirements

To be a film writer, you should be creative and able to express ideas clearly, have a broad general knowledge, be skilled in research techniques, have a love of films and film history, and be computer literate. Other assets include curiosity, persistence, initiative, resourcefulness, and an accurate memory. For some jobs—on a newspaper, for example, where the activity is hectic and deadlines are short—the ability to concentrate and produce under pressure is essential. Film critics and columnists need to be confident about their opinions and able to accept criticism from others who may not agree with their views on a film or a film-related topic.

EXPLORING

Jobs in bookstores, magazine shops, and even newsstands will offer you a chance to become familiar with various publications.

Major film publications to read include *Variety* (http://www
variety.com), *The Hollywood Reporter* (http://www.hollywood
reporter.com), *Entertainment Weekly* (http://www.ew.com), *Cinefex* (http://www.cinefex.com), *Hollywood Scriptwriter* (http://www
.hollywoodscriptwriter.com), *Animation Journal* (http://www
.animationjournal.com), and *Animation World* (http://www.awn
.com/magazines/animation-world-magazine).

As a high school or college student, you can test your interest
and aptitude in the field of writing by serving as a reporter or writer
on school newspapers, yearbooks, and literary magazines. Perhaps
you could write movie reviews for your school newspaper or an
article about a particular film genre or movement for your school's
literary magazine. There are also many Web sites where amateur
film critics can post their reviews. Of course, you can always write
movie reviews and articles on your own for practice. Small community newspapers often welcome contributions from outside sources,
although they may not have the resources to pay for them. Be sure
to take as many writing courses and workshops as you can to help
you sharpen your writing skills. You might also consider picking up
a copy of *A Short Guide to Writing About Film* (New York: Long-
man, 2009) to help you hone your writing skills.

You can also obtain information on writing as a career by visiting local newspapers and publishers and interviewing some of the
writers who work there. Career conferences and other guidance
programs frequently include speakers on the entire field of journalism from local or national organizations.

EMPLOYERS

Only about 2,000 of the approximately 151,700 writers and authors
in the United States specialize in writing about film. Many writers work for newspapers, magazines, and book publishers; radio
and television broadcasting companies; and Internet publishing and
broadcasting companies. Outside the field of journalism, writers are
also employed by advertising agencies, public relations firms, and
for journals and newsletters published by business and nonprofit
organizations, such as professional associations, labor unions,
and religious organizations. Other nonjournalism employers are
government agencies and film production companies. Other writers work as novelists, short story writers, poets, playwrights, and
screenwriters.

The major newspaper, magazine, and book publishers account
for the concentration of journalistic writers in large cities such

as New York, Chicago, Los Angeles, Boston, Philadelphia, San Francisco, and Washington, D.C. Opportunities with small publishers can be found throughout the country.

STARTING OUT

You will need a good amount of experience to gain a high-level position in the field. Nearly all film writers start out in entry-level positions. These jobs may be listed with college career services offices, or they may be obtained by applying directly to the employment departments of the individual publishers or broadcasting companies. Graduates who previously served internships with these companies often have the advantage of knowing someone who can give them a personal recommendation. Want ads in newspapers and trade journals are another source for jobs. Because of the competition for positions, however, few vacancies are listed with public or private employment agencies.

Employers in the field of journalism usually are interested in samples of published writing. These are often assembled in an organized portfolio or scrapbook. Bylined or signed articles are more credible (and, as a result, more useful) than stories whose source is not identified.

Beginning positions as a junior writer usually involve library research, preparation of rough drafts for part or all of a report, cataloging, and other related writing tasks. These are generally carried on under the supervision of a senior writer.

ADVANCEMENT

Most film writers find their first jobs as editorial, production, or research assistants. Advancement may be more rapid in small media companies, where beginners learn by doing a little bit of everything and may be given writing tasks immediately. At large publishers or broadcast companies, duties are usually more compartmentalized. Assistants in entry-level positions are assigned such tasks as research and fact checking, but it generally takes much longer to advance to full-scale writing duties.

Promotion into higher level positions may come with the assignment of more important articles and stories to write, or it may be the result of moving to another company. Mobility among employees in this field is common. A staff film writer at a small magazine publisher may switch to a similar position at a more prestigious publication.

Freelance or self-employed writers earn advancement in the form of larger fees as they gain exposure and establish their reputations.

EARNINGS

Writers who worked in the motion picture and video industries earned mean annual salaries of $85,420 in 2009, according to the U.S. Department of Labor (DOL). Salaries for all writers ranged from less than $28,070 to $105,710 or more. Writers employed by newspaper and book publishers had annual mean earnings of $53,050. Some film writers also work in radio and television broadcasting. The mean annual salary for writers employed in these industries was $65,330 in 2009.

In addition to their salaries, many film writers earn some income from freelance work. Part-time freelancers may earn from $5,000 to $15,000 a year. Freelance earnings vary widely. Full-time established freelance writers may earn $75,000 or more a year.

Benefits for full-time workers include vacation and sick time, health, and sometimes dental, insurance, and pension or 401(k) plans. Self-employed writers must provide their own benefits.

WORK ENVIRONMENT

Working conditions vary for film writers. Although their workweek usually runs 35 to 40 hours, many writers work overtime. A publication that is issued frequently has more deadlines closer together, creating greater pressures to meet them. The work is especially hectic on newspapers, which operate seven days a week. Writers often work nights and weekends to meet deadlines or to cover a late-developing story.

Most writers work independently, but they often must cooperate with editors, artists, photographers, and rewriters who may have widely differing ideas of how the materials should be prepared and presented.

Physical surroundings range from comfortable private offices to noisy, crowded newsrooms filled with other workers typing and talking on the telephone. Some writers must confine their research to the library or telephone interviews, but others may travel to movie theaters, press conferences, movie sets, award shows, or other offices.

The work is arduous, but most film writers are seldom bored. The most difficult element is the continual pressure of deadlines. People who are the most content as film writers enjoy and work well with deadline pressure.

OUTLOOK

The employment of all writers is expected to increase about as fast as the average for all occupations through 2018, according to the DOL. The demand for writers by newspapers, periodicals, and book publishers is expected to increase. The growth of online publishing will also demand many talented writers; those with computer skills will be at an advantage as a result.

People entering the field of writing, especially film writing, should realize that the competition for jobs is extremely keen. Beginners, especially, may have difficulty finding employment. Of the thousands who graduate each year with degrees in English, journalism, communications, and the liberal arts, intending to establish a career as a writer, many turn to other occupations when they find that applicants far outnumber the job openings available.

Potential film writers who end up working in a field other than journalism may be able to earn some income as freelancers, selling articles, stories, books, and possibly TV and movie scripts, but it is usually difficult for anyone to be self-supporting entirely on independent writing.

FOR MORE INFORMATION

Visit the association's Web site to learn more about the book business.

Association of American Publishers
71 Fifth Avenue, 2nd Floor
New York, NY 10003-3004
Tel: 212-255-0200
http://www.publishers.org

This organization is a good source of information about the magazine industry.

Association of Magazine Media
810 Seventh Avenue, 24th Floor
New York, NY 10019-5873
Tel: 212-872-3700
E-mail: mpa@magazine.org
http://www.magazine.org

The association represents nearly 200 television, radio, and online critics in the United States and Canada.

Broadcast Film Critics Association
Attn.: CriticsChoice.com

9220 Sunset Boulevard, Suite 220
Los Angeles, CA 90069-3503
Tel: 310-860-2665
E-mail: info@bfca.org
http://criticschoice.com/static/bfca

The following organizations represent film critics in cities across the United States.
Chicago Film Critics Association
E-mail: critics@chicagofilmcritics.org
http://www.chicagofilmcritics.org

Los Angeles Film Critics Association
http://www.lafca.net

New York Film Critics Circle
http://www.nyfcc.com

For information on the Golden Globe Awards, contact
Hollywood Foreign Press Association
646 North Robertson Boulevard
West Hollywood, CA 90069-5022
E-mail: info@hfpa.org
http://www.goldenglobes.org

For information about working as a writer and union membership, contact
National Writers Union
256 West 38th Street, Suite 703
New York, NY 10018-9807
Tel: 212-254-0279
E-mail: nwu@nwu.org
http://www.nwu.org

For information on careers in the newspaper industry, contact
Newspaper Association of America
4401 Wilson Boulevard, Suite 900
Arlington, VA 22203-1867
Tel: 571-366-1000
http://www.naa.org

The OFCS is an international association of Internet-based film critics and journalists.

Online Film Critics Society (OFCS)
E-mail: admissions@ofcs.org
http://www.ofcs.org

For a variety of journalism resources, visit the SPJ Web site.
Society of Professional Journalists (SPJ)
3909 North Meridian Street
Indianapolis, IN 46208-4011
Tel: 317-927-8000
http://www.spj.org

Visit the following Web site for detailed information about journalism careers:
High School Journalism
http://www.hsj.org

Lighting Technicians

QUICK FACTS

School Subjects
Mathematics
Technical/shop

Personal Skills
Following instructions
Mechanical/manipulative

Work Environment
Indoors and outdoors
Primarily multiple locations

Minimum Education Level
Some postsecondary training

Salary Range
$21,840 to $45,540 to
$69,020+

Certification or Licensing
None available

Outlook
About as fast as the average

DOT
962

GOE
01.08.01

NOC
5226

O*NET-SOC
27–4011.00

OVERVIEW

Lighting technicians set up and control lighting equipment for motion pictures, television broadcasts, taped television shows, and video productions. They begin by consulting with the production director and technical director to determine the types of lighting and special effects that are needed. Working with spot and flood lights, mercury-vapor lamps, white and colored lights, reflectors (mainly employed out-of-doors), and a large array of dimming, masking, and switching controls, they light scenes to be filmed or broadcast.

HISTORY

For centuries before the arrival of electric lights, theaters used candles and oil lamps to make the action on an indoor stage visible. The effects produced were necessarily limited by the lack of technology. In 1879, Thomas A. Edison developed a practical electric light bulb by removing most of the oxygen from a glass bulb and then sending current through a carbon filament inside—producing a light that would not burn out. With the arrival of electric lights, it was only a short time before theater lighting became more sophisticated; spotlights and various lighting filters were put to use, and specialists in lighting emerged.

The manipulation of light and shadow is one of the basic principles of filmmaking. This was particularly the case during the era of the silent film; without sound, filmmakers relied upon images to tell their stories. Lighting professionals learned how to make the illusion complete; through expert lighting, cardboard backdrops could substitute for the outdoors, actors could change appearance, and cheaply constructed costumes could look extravagant. Lighting technicians were the first visual effects masters, using tricks with light to achieve realism. As film techniques and equipment evolved, lighting technicians worked with cinematographers and directors to create the dark recesses and gritty streets of the film noir, the lavish spectacle of the movie musical, and the sweeping plains of the American Western, often within the confines of a studio. In the 1960s and 1970s, however, a new movie realism called for lighting technicians to expose, with uneven lighting and weak light sources, all the imperfections they'd been covering up before. Today, in the era of the special effects blockbuster, lighting technicians have gone back to their roots, using light and advanced equipment to make model cities, planets, and monsters look real.

THE JOB

Whenever a movie is filmed, the location must be well lit, whether indoors in a studio or outdoors on location. Without proper lighting, the cameras would not be able to film properly, and the show would be difficult to watch. Lighting technicians set up and control the lighting equipment for movie and television productions. These technicians are sometimes known as *assistant chief set electricians* or *lights operators*.

When beginning a project, lighting technicians consult with the director to determine the lighting effects needed; then they arrange the lighting equipment and plan the light-switching sequence that will achieve the desired effects. For example, if the script calls for sunshine to be streaming in through a window, they will set up lights to produce this effect. Other effects they may be asked to produce include lightning, the flash from an explosion, or the soft glow of a candle-lit room.

For a television series, which uses a similar format for each broadcast, the lights often remain in one fixed position for every show. For a one-time production, such as a scene in a movie, the lights have to be physically set up according to the particular scene.

During filming, lighting technicians follow a script that they have marked or follow instructions from the technical director. The script tells them which lighting effects are needed at every point in the filming. If necessary they may alter the lighting as the scene progresses by adjusting controls in the control room.

Even outdoor scenes require lighting, especially to remove shadows from people's faces. For outdoor scenes in bad weather or on rough terrain, it may be a difficult task to secure the lighting apparatus firmly so that it is out of the way, stable, and protected. During a scene, lighting technicians must be able to concentrate on the lighting of the scene and must be able to make quick, sure decisions about lighting changes.

There are different positions within this field, depending on experience. A lighting technician can move up into the position of *best boy* (the term applies to both genders). This person assists the *chief lighting technician,* or *gaffer,* as well as the *key grip.* The gaffer is the head of the lighting department and hires the lighting crew. Gaffers must be sure the filmed scene looks the way the director and the director of photography want it to look. They must diagram each scene to be filmed and determine where to position each light and decide what kinds of lights will work best for each particular scene. Gaffers must be observant, noticing dark and bright spots and correcting their light levels before filming takes place. The key grip manages all the equipment (including lights) used by the director of photography.

REQUIREMENTS

High School

You should learn as much as possible about electronics in high school. Physics, mathematics, and any shop courses that introduce electronics equipment provide a good background. You should also take courses that will help you develop computer skills needed for operating lighting and sound equipment. Composition or technical writing courses can give you the writing skills you'll need to communicate ideas to other technicians.

Postsecondary Training

There is strong competition for positions in the movie industry, and, in general, only well-prepared technicians get good jobs. You should attend a two-year postsecondary training program in electronics and broadcast technology, especially if you hope to advance to a supervisory position. Film schools also offer useful degrees in production, as do theater degrees.

Other Requirements

Setting up lights can be heavy work, especially when lighting a large movie set. You should be able to handle heavy lights on stands and work with suspended lights while on a ladder. Repairs such as changing light bulbs or replacing worn wires are sometimes necessary. You should be able to work with electricians' hand tools (screwdrivers, pliers, and so forth) and be comfortable working with electricity.

You should also be dependable and capable of working as part of a team. Communication skills, both listening and speaking, are necessary when working with a director and with assistant lighting technicians.

EXPLORING

Valuable learning experiences for prospective lighting technicians include working on the lighting for a school stage production, building a radio from a kit, or a summer job in an appliance or TV or computer repair shop. High school shop or vocational teachers may be able to arrange a presentation by a qualified lighting technician.

You can also learn a lot about the technical side of production by operating a camera for your school's journalism or media department. Recording a play, concert, or sporting event will give you additional insight into production work. You may also have the opportunity to intern or volunteer with a local technical crew for a film or TV production. Check the Internet for production schedules, or volunteer to work for your state's film commission where you'll hear about area projects.

EMPLOYERS

Many lighting technicians work on a freelance basis, taking on film, TV, and commercial projects as they come along. Technicians can find full-time work with large theater companies and television broadcast stations, or any organization, such as a museum or sports arena, that requires special lighting. Lighting technicians also work for video production companies.

STARTING OUT

The best way to get experience is to find a position as an intern. Offering to work on a production for course credit or experience instead of pay will enable you to learn about the job and to establish valuable connections. Most people interested in film enter the industry as production assistants. These positions are often unpaid and require a great deal of time and work with little reward. However, production assistants have the opportunity to network with people in the industry. They get to speak to lighting technicians and to see them at work. Once they have worked on a few productions, and have learned many of the basics of lighting, they can negotiate for paid positions on future projects.

ADVANCEMENT

An experienced lighting technician will be able to move up into the position of best boy. With a few more years' experience working under different gaffers on diverse projects, the technician may move into the position of gaffer or chief lighting technician. Gaffers command greater salaries as they gain experience working with many different cinematographers. Many experienced technicians join the International Alliance of Theatrical Stage Employees, Moving Picture Technicians, Artists and Allied Crafts (IATSE) of the United States, Its Territories, and Canada as lighting technicians or studio mechanics; union membership is required for work on major productions. Some lighting technicians go on to work as cinematographers, or to make their own films or television movies.

EARNINGS

Salaries for lighting technicians vary according to the technician's experience. Annual income is also determined by the number of projects a technician is hired for; the most experienced technicians can work year-round on a variety of projects, while those starting out may go weeks without work. Audio and video equipment technicians (a category that includes those who work with lighting) earned salaries that ranged from less than $21,840 to $69,020 or more in 2009, according to the U.S. Department of Labor (DOL). Those employed in the motion picture and video industries had mean annual earnings of $45,540. Experienced technicians can negotiate for much higher wages. Union members receive health and retirement benefits.

WORK ENVIRONMENT

Lighting technicians who work in the motion picture industry are often employed for one production at a time and thus may work less regularly and under a more challenging variety of conditions than light technicians in television studio work.

Technicians often work long days, especially when a film is on a tight schedule. Technicians may travel a good deal to be on location for filming. They work both indoors in studios and outdoors on location, under a variety of weather conditions.

OUTLOOK

The DOL predicts that employment for audio and video equipment technicians (a category that includes lighting technicians) will grow about as fast as the average for all careers through 2018. As long as the movie and television industries continue to grow, opportunities will remain available for people who wish to become lighting technicians. With the expansion of the cable and satellite television market, lighting technicians may find work in more than one area. However, persistence and hard work are required in order to secure a good job in film or television.

The increasing use of visual effects and computer-generated imagery (CGI) will likely have an impact on the work of lighting technicians. Through computer programs, filmmakers and editors can adjust lighting themselves; however, live-action shots are still integral to the filmmaking process, and will remain so for some time. To get the initial shots of a film will require sophisticated lighting equipment and trained technicians. Lighting technicians often have to know about the assembly and operation of more pieces of equipment than anyone else working on a production. Equipment will become more compact and mobile, making the technician's job easier.

FOR MORE INFORMATION

For information about colleges with film and television programs of study, and to read interviews with filmmakers, visit the AFI Web site.

American Film Institute (AFI)
2021 North Western Avenue
Los Angeles, CA 90027-1657
Tel: 323-856-7600
E-mail: information@afi.com
http://www.afi.com

Visit the ASC Web site for a great deal of valuable insight into the industry, including interviews with award-winning cinematographers, a "tricks of the trade" page, information about film schools, multimedia presentations, and articles from American Cinematographer *magazine.*

American Society of Cinematographers (ASC)
PO Box 2230
Hollywood, CA 90078-2230
Tel: 800-448-0145
E-mail: office@theasc.com
http://www.theasc.com

For education and training information, contact
International Alliance of Theatrical Stage Employees, Moving Picture Technicians, Artists and Allied Crafts of the United States, Its Territories, and Canada
1430 Broadway, 20th Floor
New York, NY 10018-3348
Tel: 212-730-1770
http://www.iatse-intl.org

For information on union membership for lighting technicians, contact
IATSE-Local 728
1001 West Magnolia Boulevard
Burbank, CA 91506-1606
Tel: 818-891-0728
http://www.iatse728.org

Media Planners and Buyers

OVERVIEW

Media specialists are responsible for placing advertisements that will reach targeted customers and get the best response from the market for the least amount of money. Within the media department, *media planners* gather information about the sizes and types of audiences that can be reached through each of the various media and about the cost of advertising in each medium. *Media buyers,* sometimes called *advertising sales agents,* purchase space in printed publications, time on radio or television stations, and ads on the Internet. Advertising media workers are supervised by a *media director,* who is accountable for the overall media plan. In addition to advertising agencies, media planners and buyers work for large companies that purchase space or broadcast time. There are approximately 166,800 advertising sales agents employed in the United States.

HISTORY

The first formal media that allowed advertisers to deliver messages about their products or services to the public were newspapers and magazines, which began selling space to advertisers in the late 19th century. This system of placing ads gave rise to the first media planners and buyers, who were in charge of deciding what kind of advertising to put in which publications and then actually purchasing the space.

In the broadcast realm, radio stations started offering program time to advertisers in the early 1900s. And, while television advertising began just before the end of World War II, producers were quick to realize that they could reach huge audiences by placing ads on TV. Television advertising proved to be beneficial to the TV stations as well, since they relied on sponsors for financial assistance in order to bring programs into people's homes. In the past, programs were sometimes named not for the host or star of the program, but for the sponsoring company that was paying for the broadcast of that particular show.

During the early years of radio and television, it was often possible for one sponsor to pay for an entire 30-minute program. The cost of producing shows on radio and television, however, increased dramatically, requiring many sponsors to support a single radio or television program. Media planners and buyers learned to get more for their money by buying smaller amounts of time—60-, 30-, and even 10-second spots—on a greater number of programs.

Today's media planners and buyers have a wide array of media from which to choose. The newest of these, the Internet, allows advertisers not only to precisely target customers but to interact with them as well. In addition to Web banner ads, producers can also advertise via sponsorships, their own Web sites, social networking sites such as Facebook, blogs, microblogging sites such as Twitter, voice-mail telephone shopping, and more. With so many choices, media planners and buyers must carefully determine target markets and select the ideal media mix in order to reach these markets at the least cost.

THE JOB

While many employees may work in the media department, the primary specialists are the media planner and the media buyer. They work with professionals from a wide range of media—from billboards, direct mail, and magazines to television, radio, and the Internet. Both types of media specialists must be familiar with the markets that each medium reaches, as well as the advantages and disadvantages of advertising in each.

Media planners determine target markets based on their clients' advertising approaches. Considering their clients' products and services, budget, and image, media planners gather information about the public's viewing, reading, and buying habits by administering questionnaires and conducting other forms of market research. Through this research, planners are able to identify target markets by sorting data according to people's ages, incomes, marital status, interests, and leisure activities.

By knowing which groups of people watch certain shows, listen to specific radio stations, or read particular magazines or newspapers, media planners can help clients select airtime or print space to reach the consumers most likely to buy their products. For example, Saturday morning television shows attract children, while late-night programs often draw young singles. For shows broadcast at these times, media planners will recommend airtime to their clients who are interested in advertising a certain type of movie to these viewers, such as an animated film or an R-rated comedy, respectively.

Media planners who work directly for companies selling airtime or print space must be sensitive to their clients' budgets and resources. When tailoring their sales pitch to a particular client's needs, planners often go to great lengths to persuade the client to buy airtime or advertising space. They produce brochures and reports that detail the characteristics of their viewing or reading market, including the average income of those individuals, the number of people who see the ads, and any other information that may be likely to encourage potential advertisers to promote their products.

Media planners try to land contracts by inviting clients to meetings and presentations and educating them about various marketing strategies. They must not only pursue new clients but also attend to current ones, making sure that they are happy with their existing advertising packages. For both new and existing clients, the media planner's main objective is to sell as much airtime or ad space as possible.

Media buyers do the actual purchasing of the time on radio or television or the space in a newspaper or magazine in which an advertisement will run. In addition to tracking the time and space available for purchase, media buyers ensure that ads appear when and where they should, negotiate costs for ad placement, and calculate rates, usage, and budgets. They also maintain contact with clients, keeping them informed of all advertising-related developments and resolving any conflicts that arise. Large companies that generate a lot of advertising or those that place only print ads or only broadcast ads sometimes differentiate between the two main media groups by employing *space buyers* and/or *time buyers*.

Workers who actually sell the print space or airtime to advertisers are called *print sales workers* or *broadcast time salespeople*. Like media planners, these professionals are well versed about the target markets served by their organizations and can often provide useful information about editorial content or broadcast programs.

In contrast to print and broadcast planners and buyers, *interactive media specialists* manage all critical aspects of their clients' online advertising campaigns. While interactive media planners may have responsibilities similar to those of print or broadcast planners, they also act as new technology specialists, placing and tracking all online ads and maintaining relationships with clients and Webmasters alike.

The typical online media planning process begins with an agency spreadsheet that details the criteria about the media buy. These criteria often include target demographics, start and end dates for the ad campaign, and online objectives. After sending all relevant information to a variety of Web sites, the media specialist receives cost, market, and other data from the sites. Finally, the media specialist places the order and sends all creative information needed to the selected Web sites. Once the order has been placed, the media specialist receives tracking and performance data and then compiles and analyzes the information in preparation for future ad campaigns.

Media planners and buyers may have a wide variety of clients. Film studios, television networks, restaurants, hotel chains, beverage companies, food product manufacturers, and automobile dealers all need to advertise to attract potential customers. While huge companies, such as motion picture studios, soft drink manufacturers, major airlines, and vacation resorts, pay a lot of money to have their products or services advertised nationally, many smaller firms need to advertise only in their immediate area. Local advertising may come from a health club that wants to announce a special membership rate or from a retail store promoting a sale. Media planners and buyers must be aware of their various clients' advertising needs and create campaigns that will accomplish their promotional objectives.

REQUIREMENTS
High School
Although most media positions, including those at the entry level, require a bachelor's degree, you can prepare for a future job as media planner and/or buyer by taking specific courses offered at the high school level. These include business, computer science, marketing, advertising, cinematography, radio and television, and film and video. General liberal arts classes, such as economics, English, communication, and journalism, are also important, since media planners and buyers must be able to communicate clearly with both clients and coworkers. In addition, mathematics classes will give you the skills to work accurately with budget figures and placement costs.

Postsecondary Training

Increasingly, media planners and buyers have college degrees, often with majors in marketing or advertising. Even if you have prior work experience or training in media, you should select college classes that provide a good balance of business course work, broadcast and print experience, and liberal arts studies.

Business classes may include economics, marketing, sales, and advertising. In addition, courses that focus on specific media, such as cinematography, film and video, radio and television, and new technologies (like the Internet), are important. Additional classes in journalism, English, and speech will prove helpful as well. Media directors often need to have a master's degree, as well as extensive experience working with the various media.

Other Requirements

Media planners and buyers in broadcasting should have a keen understanding of programming and consumer buying trends, as well as a knowledge of each potential client's business. Print media specialists must be familiar with the process involved in creating print ads and the markets reached by various publications. Those who specialize in the Internet should have knowledge of technology and the types of advertisements and marketing approaches that work best online. In addition, all media workers need to be capable of maintaining good relationships with current clients, as well as pursuing new clients on a continual basis.

Communication and problem-solving skills are important, as are creativity, common sense, patience, and persistence. Media planners and buyers must also have excellent oral, written, and analytical skills; knowledge of interactive media planning trends and tools; and the ability to handle multiple assignments in a fast-paced work environment. Strategic thinking skills, industry interest, and computer experience with both database and word processing programs are also vital.

EXPLORING

Many high schools and two-year colleges and most four-year colleges have media departments that may include radio stations and public access or cable television channels. In order to gain worthwhile experience in media, you can work for these departments as aides, production assistants, programmers, or writers. In addition, high school and college newspapers and yearbooks often need students to sell advertising to local merchants. Theater departments also frequently look for people to sell ads for performance programs.

In the local community, newspapers and other publications often hire high school students to work part time and/or in the summer in sales and clerical positions for the classified advertising department. Some towns have cable television stations that regularly look for volunteers to operate cameras, sell advertising, and coordinate various programs. In addition, a variety of religious-sponsored activities, such as craft fairs, holiday boutiques, and rummage sales, can provide you with opportunities to create and place ads and work with the local media in order to get exposure for the events.

EMPLOYERS

Media planners and buyers often work for advertising agencies in large cities, such as Chicago, New York, and Los Angeles. These agencies represent various clients who are trying to sell everything from financial services to dishwasher soap to the latest comedy featuring the hot star of the moment. Other media specialists work directly for radio and television networks, newspapers, magazines, and Web sites selling airtime and ad space. While many of these media organizations are located in large urban areas, particularly radio and television stations, most small towns have newspapers and therefore need specialists to sell ad space and coordinate accounts. Approximately 166,800 advertising sales agents work in the United States. Thirty-three percent are employed in advertising, public relations, and related services. Thirty-two percent work for newspaper, book, periodical, and directory publishers, and 17 percent of agents work in radio and television broadcasting.

STARTING OUT

More than half of the jobs in print and broadcast media do not remain open long enough for companies to advertise available positions in the classified sections of newspapers. As a result, many media organizations, such as radio and television stations, do not usually advertise job openings in the want ads. Media planners and buyers often hear about available positions through friends, acquaintances, or family members and frequently enter the field as entry-level broadcasting or sales associates. Both broadcasting and sales can provide employees just starting out with experience in approaching and working for clients, as well as knowledge about the specifics of programming and its relation to selling airtime.

Advertising agencies sometimes do advertise job openings, both in local and national papers and on the Web. Competition is quite fierce for entry-level jobs, however, particularly at large agencies in big cities.

Print media employees often start working on smaller publications as in-house sales staff members, answering telephones and taking orders from customers. Other duties may include handling classified ads or coordinating the production and placement of small print ads created by in-house artists. While publications often advertise for entry-level positions, the best way to find work in advertising is to send resumes to as many agencies, publications, and broadcasting offices as possible. With any luck, your resume will arrive just as an opening is becoming available.

While you are enrolled in a college program, you should investigate opportunities for internships or on-campus employment in related areas. Your school's career planning center or placement office should have information on such positions. Previous experience often provides a competitive edge for all job seekers, but it is crucial to aspiring media planners and buyers.

ADVANCEMENT

Large agencies and networks often hire only experienced people, so it is common for media planners and buyers to learn the business at smaller companies. These opportunities allow media specialists to gain the experience and confidence they need to move up to more advanced positions. Jobs at smaller agencies and television and radio stations also provide possibilities for more rapid promotion than those at larger organizations.

Media planners and buyers climbing the company ladder can advance to the position of media director or may earn promotions to executive-level positions. For those already at the management level, advancement can come in the form of larger clients and more responsibility. In addition, many media planners and buyers who have experience with traditional media are investigating the opportunities and challenges that come with the job of interactive media planner/buyer or Web media specialist.

EARNINGS

Because media planners and buyers work for a variety of organizations all across the country and abroad, earnings can vary greatly. Media planners earned salaries that ranged from less than $37,537 to $62,961 or more in 2011, according to Salary.com. Earnings for media buyers ranged from less than $39,810 to more than $79,245.

Media planners and buyers in television typically earn higher salaries than those in radio. In general, however, beginning broadcasting salespeople usually earn between $18,000 and $35,000 per year and can advance to as much as $50,000 after a few years of experience.

According to the U.S. Department of Labor (DOL), advertising sales agents earned salaries that ranged from less than $22,610 to more than $94,100 in 2009. Advertising sales agents employed in the motion picture and video industries earned $66,840.

Most employers of media planners and buyers offer a variety of benefits, including health and life insurance, a retirement plan, and paid vacation and sick days.

WORK ENVIRONMENT

Although media planners and buyers often work a 40-hour week, their hours are not strictly nine to five. Service calls, presentations, and meetings with ad space reps and clients are important parts of the job that usually have a profound effect on work schedules. In addition, media planners and buyers must invest considerable time investigating and reading about trends in programming, buying, and advertising.

The variety of opportunities for media planners and buyers results in a wide diversity of working conditions. Larger advertising agencies, publications, and networks may have modern and comfortable working facilities. Smaller markets may have more modest working environments.

Whatever the size of the organization, many planners seldom go into the office and must call in to keep in touch with the home organization. Travel is a big part of media planners' responsibilities to their clients, and they may have clients in many different types of businesses and services, as well as in different areas of the country.

While much of the media planner and buyer's job requires interaction with a variety of people, including coworkers, sales reps, supervisors, and clients, most media specialists also perform many tasks that require independent work, such as researching and writing reports. In any case, the media planner and buyer must be able to handle many tasks at the same time in a fast-paced, continually changing environment.

OUTLOOK

The employment outlook for media planners and buyers, like the outlook for the advertising industry itself, depends on the general health of the economy. When the economy thrives, companies produce an increasing number of goods and seek to promote them via television, radio, the Internet, newspapers, magazines, and various other media. The DOL predicts that employment in the advertising industry will grow 8 percent over the 2008–18 period, about as fast as the average for all industries.

More and more people are relying on radio and television for their entertainment and information. With cable and local television channels offering a wide variety of programs, advertisers are increasingly turning to TV in order to get exposure for their products and services. Although newspaper sales are in decline, there is growth in special interest periodicals and other print publications. Interactive media, such as the Internet, are providing a flurry of advertising activity all around the world. All of this activity will increase market opportunities for media planners and buyers.

Employment possibilities for media specialists are far greater in large cities, such as New York, Los Angeles, and Chicago, where most magazines and many broadcast networks have their headquarters. However, smaller publications are often located in outlying areas, and large national organizations usually have sales offices in several cities across the country.

Competition for all advertising positions, including entry-level jobs, is expected to be intense. Media planners and buyers who have considerable experience will have the best chances of finding employment.

FOR MORE INFORMATION

For profiles of advertising workers and career information, contact

Advertising Educational Foundation
220 East 42nd Street, Suite 3300
New York, NY 10017-5806
Tel: 212-986-8060
http://www.aef.com

For information on college chapters, internship opportunities, and financial aid opportunities, contact

American Advertising Federation
1101 Vermont Avenue, NW, Suite 500
Washington, DC 20005-6306
Tel: 800-999-2231
E-mail: aaf@aaf.org
http://www.aaf.org

For information on advertising agencies, contact
American Association of Advertising Agencies
405 Lexington Avenue, 18th Floor
New York, NY 10174-1801
Tel: 212-682-2500
http://www.aaaa.org

For career resources and job listings, contact
American Marketing Association
311 South Wacker Drive, Suite 5800
Chicago, IL 60606-6629
Tel: 800-262-1150
http://www.marketingpower.com

For information on education and training, contact
Marketing Research Association
110 National Drive, 2nd Floor
Glastonbury, CT 06033-4372
Tel: 860-682-1000
E-mail: email@mra-net.org
http://www.mra-net.org

Producers

OVERVIEW

Producers organize and secure the financial backing for the production of motion pictures and television shows. They decide which scripts will be used or which books will be adapted for film or a television show. Producers also raise money to finance the filming of a production; hire the director, screenwriter, and cast; oversee the budget and production schedule; and monitor the distribution of the film. Approximately 4,000 motion picture, television, and new media producers are members of the Producers Guild of America.

HISTORY

Motion picture cameras were invented in the late 1800s. The two earliest known films, made in 1888 by French-born Louis Le Prince, showed his father-in-law's garden and traffic crossing an English bridge.

More advanced cameras and motion picture techniques quickly followed. In 1903, American director Edwin Porter and inventor Thomas Edison made *The Great Train Robbery,* one of the first movies in which scenes were filmed out of sequence; when the filming was completed, the scenes were edited and spliced together. By 1906 feature-length films were being made and many talented and financially savvy individuals were making their livings as producers. The first woman to become a producer was Alice Guy, who started the Solax Company in New York in 1910.

In 1911, the Centaur Company, which had been trying to film westerns in New Jersey, moved to California and became the first studio to settle in Hollywood. Many film companies followed the lead of Centaur and moved their operations to Southern California where there was abundant sunshine and a variety of terrain.

The film industry began to consolidate in the late 1920s after the introduction of sound films and the 1929 stock market crash. Small and marginally profitable producers were forced out of business. This left the largest companies, which controlled most of the first-run theaters, to dominate the market. Major studios produced their films in a factory-like fashion. With their permanent staff of cameramen and other technical workers, a major studio could produce 40 or more films annually. And because many of the larger studios also owned their own network of theaters throughout the United States, they had a guaranteed market to which they could distribute their films. This stable, mass-produced system gave some studios the encouragement to produce commercially risky art films as well.

In 1945, following World War II, commercial television broadcasting became available in the United States. The television industry experienced phenomenal growth through increasingly better equipment, more TV stations, and larger audiences. Television was partly responsible for a decline in the number of theatergoers, causing financial difficulties for the film studios. An antitrust court judgment against the studios also eliminated their dominance of the movie theater market. But with the emergence and growth of television, and a steady need for new shows and made-for-TV films, television broadened employment opportunities for producers. The major studios experienced financial difficulties in the 1950s, which because of studio downsizing and other pressures, led to a growth in the number of independent producers. Changes in the U.S. tax code made independent producing even more profitable. In response to their financial difficulties, studios began to reduce the number of films produced each year and to rely more on expensive "blockbuster" films to attract audiences.

In the early 1970s, the industry again went through a major reorganization. The staggering expense of producing blockbusters had drained the major studios of their profits, and these financially strapped companies began to make films under strict cost-containment measures. This led to an increase of independent producers initiating film projects. Today, while independent movies remain popular, big-budget blockbuster movies produce the highest box office revenues.

Technical innovations have had great influence on motion picture producing. Portable lights, cameras, and other equipment allow films to be made anywhere and reduce the dependence on studio sets. More recently, the emergence of cable television and the growing

Interesting College Program

Interested in learning how to become a producer by attending college? If so, the graduate-level Producers Program at the University of California–Los Angeles's Department of Film, TV, and Digital Media might be a good place to start. Its faculty consists of respected producers, studio executives, agents, lawyers, and others involved in the motion picture and television industries. What type of classes do students involved in the program take? The following is a list of recent courses offered by the program:

- Introduction to the Art and Business of Producing
- Producing the Trailer
- Feature Film Marketing
- New Technologies for the Independent Producer
- International Financing/Co-Production
- Planning the Independent Feature Production
- Studios vs. Independents: Navigating the Process
- Entertainment Law and Business Practices
- Life After the Studio System
- The Independent Spirit: Creative Strategies
- Entertainment Management: What Makes a Hit
- Sports Entertainment
- Producing Boot Camp
- TV Development
- Special Studies: Who Really Represents Me

For more information on the program, contact
   University of California–Los Angeles
   School of Theater, Film and Television
   Department of Film, TV, and Digital Media
   Producers Program
   102 East Melnitz Hall, Box 951622
   Los Angeles, CA 90095-1622
   Tel: 310-825-5761
   E-mail: info@tft.ucla.edu
   http://www.tft.ucla.edu/producers/start.htm

number of platforms to view movies (such as the Internet, MP3 players, smart phones, and personal computers) have created demand for more content and opened new markets for film producers. Advances in computer technology have also created a renaissance in animation.

Animated films such as *WALL-E* and *Up* have been some of the most popular movies of recent years. High-quality animation is also being created for adults. One example of an adult-oriented animated film is *Waltz with Bashir*, which was nominated for an Academy Award in 2008.

In recent years, the traditional distinctions between television and movie production, as well as between American and foreign films, have become increasingly blurred. Americans finance many foreign-made films and a number of American motion picture companies are owned by foreigners.

THE JOB

The primary role of a producer is to organize and secure the financial backing necessary to undertake a motion picture project. The *director,* by contrast, creates the film from the screenplay. Despite this general distinction, the producer often takes part in creative decisions, and occasionally one person is both the producer and director. On some small projects, such as a nature or historical documentary for limited theatrical release or public television broadcast, the producer might also be the writer and cameraman.

The job of a film producer generally begins in the preproduction stage of filmmaking with the selection of a movie idea from a script, or other material. Some films are made from original screenplays, while others are adapted from video games and books. If a video game or book is selected, the producer must first purchase the rights from the author or his or her publishing company or the game development company, and a writer must be hired to adapt the book or video game into a screenplay format. Producers are usually inundated with scripts from writers and others who have ideas for a movie. Producers may have their own ideas for a motion picture and will hire a writer to write the screenplay. Occasionally a studio will approach a producer, typically a producer who has had many commercially or artistically successful films in the past, with a project.

After selecting a project, the producer will find a director, the technical staff, and the star actor or actors to participate in the film. Along with the script and screenwriter, these essential people are referred to as the package. Packaging is sometimes arranged with the help of talent agencies. It is the package that the producer tries to sell to an investor to obtain the necessary funds to finance the salaries and cost of the film.

There are three common sources for financing a film: major studios, production companies, and individual investors. A small number of producers have enough money to pay for their own projects. Major studios are the largest source of money, and finance most of the big-budget films. Although some studios have full-time producers on staff, they hire self-employed, or *independent producers*, for many projects. Large production companies often have the capital resources to fund projects that they feel will be commercially successful. On the smaller end of the scale, producers of documentary films commonly approach individual donors; foundations; art agencies of federal, state, and local governments; and even family members and churches and other religious organizations. The National Endowment for the Humanities and the National Endowment for the Arts are major federal benefactors of cinema.

Raising money from individual investors can occupy much of the producer's time. Fund-raising may be done on the telephone, as well as in conferences, business lunches, and even cocktail parties. The producer may also look for a distributor for the film even before the production begins.

Obtaining the necessary financing does not guarantee that a film will be made. After raising the money, the producer takes the basic plan of the package and tries to work it into a developed project. The script may be rewritten several times, the full cast of actors is hired, salaries are negotiated, and logistical problems, such as the location of the filming, are worked out; on some projects it might be the director who handles these tasks, or the director may work with the producer. Most major film projects do not get beyond this complicated stage of development.

During the production phase, the producer tries to keep the project on schedule and the spending within the established budget. Other production tasks include the review of dailies, which are copies of the day's filming. They are typically transferred to digital or nonlinear format for review by directors, producers, and editors. As the head of the project, the producer is ultimately responsible for resolving all problems, including personal conflicts such as those between the director and an actor and the director and the studio. If the film is successfully completed, the producer monitors its distribution and may participate in the publicity and advertising of the film.

To accomplish the many and varied tasks that the position requires, producers hire a number of subordinates, such as *associate producers,* sometimes called *coproducers, line producers,* and *production assistants.* Job titles, however, vary from project to project. In general, associate producers work directly under the producer and oversee the major areas of the project, such as the budget. Line producers handle the day-to-day operations of the project. Production assistants may perform substantive tasks, such as reviewing scripts, but others are hired to run errands. Another title, *executive producer*, often refers to the person who puts up the money, such as a studio executive, but it is sometimes an honorary title with no functional relevance to the project.

Documentary producers are also very actively involved in their productions, but they typically have days, rather than hours, to complete projects. They may be involved in deciding on a concept for the documentary; hiring writers, directors, and the crew; and scouting out locations and finding interview subjects. Once interviews and other segments are recorded, they may review the material, select the best footage, and edit it into a program of predetermined length.

REQUIREMENTS

There is no minimum educational requirement for becoming a producer. Many producers, however, are college graduates, and many also have a business degree or other previous business experience. They must not only be talented salespeople and administrators but also have a thorough understanding of film and motion picture technology. Such understanding, of course, only comes from experience.

High School

High school courses that will be of assistance to you in your work as a producer include speech, mathematics, business, psychology, and English. Take computer science classes so that you can develop a familiarity with this tool. If your high school offers any classes on the history of film, be sure to take those. You should also consider taking drama classes that will give you an understanding of scripts and working with actors.

Postsecondary Training

Formal study of film, television, communications, theater, writing, English literature, or art is helpful, as the producer must have the background to know whether an idea or script is worth pursuing. Many entry-level positions in the film industry are given to people who have studied liberal arts, cinema, or both.

In the United States there are more than 1,000 colleges, universities, and trade schools that offer classes in film or television studies; more than 120 of these offer undergraduate programs, and more than 50 grant master's degrees. A small number of Ph.D. programs also exist.

Graduation from a film or television program does not guarantee employment in the industry. Some programs are quite expensive, costing more than $50,000 in tuition alone for three years of study.

Educational programs in Los Angeles and New York City, the major centers of the entertainment industry, may provide the best opportunities for making contacts that can be of benefit when seeking employment.

A number of organizations provide information on internships or sponsor internship programs. For example, the Directors Guild of America sponsors Los Angeles- and New York-based training programs for a limited number of college graduates. The trainees in this program are paid and work on television series projects. (See the end of this article for contact information to learn more about these opportunities.)

Other Requirements

Producers come from a wide variety of backgrounds. Some start out as magazine editors, business school graduates, actors, or secretaries, messengers, and production assistants for a film studio. Many have never formally studied film.

Most producers, however, get their position through several years of experience in the industry, perseverance, and a keen sense for what projects will be artistically and commercially successful.

The successful producer is an organized individual who can deal quickly and effectively with problems that may cause a change in production plans. Producers need to have a good sense of what stories, news, or other items will interest viewers. They also need salesmanship qualities since they may have to "sell" a station or studio on a project idea or convince an actor to take a role. Producers work with teams of professionals and must be able to bring people together to work on the single goal of completing a project.

EXPLORING

There are many ways to gain experience in filmmaking. Some high schools have film and video clubs, for example, or courses on the use of motion picture equipment. Experience in high school or college theater can also be useful. One of the best ways to get experience is to volunteer for a student or low-budget film project; positions on such projects are often advertised in local trade publications. Community cable stations also hire volunteers and may even offer internships. To meet professionals in the field, ask your media department teacher or school counselor to arrange for a movie or television producer to come talk to interested students.

EMPLOYERS

Many producers in the field are self-employed. Others are salaried employees of film companies, television networks, and television stations. Approximately 4,000 motion picture, television, and new media producers are members of the Producers Guild of America. The greatest concentration of motion picture producers is in Hollywood and New York City. About 21 percent of producers are self-employed.

STARTING OUT

Becoming a producer is similar to becoming president of a company. Unless a person is independently wealthy and can finance whichever projects he or she chooses, prior experience in the field is necessary. Because there are so few positions, even with experience it is extremely difficult to become a successful producer.

Most motion picture producers have attained their position only after years of moving up the industry ladder. Thus, it is important to concentrate on immediate goals, such as getting an entry-level position in a film company. Some enter the field by getting a job as a production assistant. An entry-level production assistant may photocopy scripts for actors to use, assist in setting up equipment, or may perform other menial tasks, often for very little or even no pay. While a production assistant's work is often tedious and of little seeming reward, it nevertheless does expose one to the intricacies of filmmaking and, more importantly, creates an opportunity to make contacts with others in the industry.

Those interested in the field should approach film companies, television stations, or the television networks about employment opportunities as a production assistant. Positions may also be listed in trade publications.

ADVANCEMENT

There is little room for advancement because producers are at the top of their profession. Advancement for producers is generally measured by the types of projects they do, increased earnings, and respect in the field. Some producers become directors or make enough money to finance their own projects.

EARNINGS

Producers are generally paid a percentage of the project's profits or a fee negotiated between the producer and a studio. According to the U.S. Department of Labor (DOL), producers and directors in the motion picture and video industries earned mean annual salaries of $108,580 in 2009. Salaries for all producers ranged from less than $30,560 to $166,400 or more.

Producers of highly successful films can earn $200,000 or more, while those who make low-budget, documentary films might earn considerably less than the average.

Producers who are full-time, salaried employees of studios typically receive benefits such as health insurance and paid vacation and sick days. Independent producers must provide these extras for themselves.

WORK ENVIRONMENT

Producers have greater control over their working conditions than most other people working in the motion picture industry. They may have the autonomy of choosing their own projects, setting their own hours, and delegating duties to others as necessary. The work often brings considerable personal satisfaction. But it is not without constraints. Producers must work within a stressful schedule complicated by competing work pressures and often daily crises. Each project brings a significant financial and professional risk. Long hours and weekend work are common. Most producers must provide for their own health insurance and other benefits.

OUTLOOK

Employment for producers who work in the motion picture and video industries is expected to grow about as fast as the average for all careers through 2018, according to the DOL. Though opportunities have grown as a result of the expansion of cable and satellite television, development of interactive media, increases in video and DVD rentals, and an increased overseas demand for American-made films, competition for jobs will remain high. Freelance opportunities are also expected to increase as networks look to independent production companies for more programming. Some positions will be available as current producers leave the workforce.

FOR MORE INFORMATION

For more information on the industry and training programs, contact
Directors Guild of America
7920 Sunset Boulevard
Los Angeles, CA 90046-3304
Tel: 310-289-2000
http://www.dga.org

For industry news and career information, contact
Producers Guild of America
8530 Wilshire Boulevard, Suite 450
Beverly Hills, CA 90211-3115
Tel: 310-358-9020
E-mail: info@producersguild.org
http://www.producersguild.org

Women in Film's mission is to "empower, promote, and mentor women in the entertainment and media industries." Visit its Web site to learn about membership, internships, competitions, and financial aid for college students.
Women in Film
6100 Wilshire Boulevard, Suite 710
Los Angeles, CA 90048-5107
Tel: 323-935-2211
E-mail: info@wif.org
http://www.wif.org

INTERVIEW

Alan Salzenstein coordinates the Performing Arts Management Program for DePaul University's School of Music and The Theatre School, and heads the MFA/Arts Leadership Program at The Theatre School at DePaul University in Chicago, Illinois. He is also a theatrical producer, consultant, and attorney. Alan discussed the field of performing arts management with the editors of Careers in Focus: Film.

Q. What is one thing young people may not know about a career in performing arts management?

A. People who follow a career in performing arts management typically have the drive and passion to work in the arts, to work in culture, but also have the business skills to support it. They have the need to be part of the arts, but can make sure it is created properly and have the audience. Those who are interested in theater administration or performing arts management, or producing theater, realize that it is a business. There definitely is a market out there for people with a business mind and the skills for producing theater.

Q. **Can you give an overview of the MFA/Arts Leadership program?**

A. It is a unique program, a dual program which combines the academic approach of learning and being a part of the commerce and the business side of culture. But it is also very hands-on. It also involves a full-time work experience in an arts organization in Chicago. It is very different from other programs because it focuses on the academic and the work experience at the same time. It is a two-year program—a sort of super internship. It's full-time work—in partnership with Chicago Shakespeare Theater. The students in the MFA program are also full-time employees at the theater, complete with benefits and specific roles in the organization. They work full-time at the theater, along with taking course work at DePaul.

Q. **Can you provide an overview of the Performing Arts Management Program?**

A. This is an undergraduate program. Ideally, it focuses on helping students work in the business side of the industry—to develop the business and management skills within a creative environment. It is also very entrepreneurial in nature—you need to be able to create the environment appropriate for the creation of theater, dance, or music.

Q. **What are some of the classes offered in this program?**

A. It is a very intensive program in terms of management and business skills in conjunction with DePaul University's College of Commerce. Our students may be enrolled in classes side by side with students majoring in business, management, or accounting. However there are also specific courses that center on performing arts management—taking business skills and learning within the context of what the arts have to offer. There are classes on marketing of the arts, fundraising and development, and working with the board of directors of an arts or theater company.

Q. What type of students enroll in these programs?

A. There are quite a variety of students. Most have a passion for the arts or perhaps have had experience in the theater in the past. Many have the understanding that their abilities are on the business side, but have the desire to support the arts and know the importance of the arts. They have a wide of variety of backgrounds—very diverse. We draw from all four corners of the country. Part of this is because Chicago is such a center for theater and culture. DePaul uses Chicago as its extended campus, and we also have connections and cooperative agreements with many of the institutions of arts and theater in the city. It is a tremendous advantage to study in this city. Chicago is such a thriving theater community and cultural center—we are able to access all this for our students.

Q. What is a typical career path for students in your programs?

A. Probably as diverse as the students who come in! Our students go on to many management positions in theater or performing arts organizations. They may be involved in marketing or development, producing in both the commercial or not-for-profit areas. Some go on to earn advanced degrees. Others go on for degrees in law or MBAs. Still others pursue advanced degrees in arts administration. Our program opens the door beyond the name of the degree—skills learned here are transferable to other areas.

Q. What are the most important personal and professional qualities for performing arts management students?

A. Qualities that I look for in potential students include the desire to learn and definitely an appreciation for the arts. This doesn't necessarily mean they have to be performers. They may have a strong background with the technical side. They should have open minds and analytical skills. Ultimately, they should have excellent communication skills. They have to be able to understand the importance of communication within the world we live in—on the business side, and very much so in the artistic world. It's important for students to be able to communicate verbally and in writing. It's also important to be able to understand the temperaments of all the personalities we have to deal with.

Production Assistants

OVERVIEW

Production assistants (PAs) perform a variety of tasks for film, television, and video producers and other staff members. They must be prepared to help out everywhere, ensuring that daily operations run as smoothly as possible. Some production assistants may perform substantive jobs, such as reviewing scripts, but others may primarily run errands. They must be willing to work hard and keep long hours at times, since tight production schedules require full days. An agreeable temperament and willingness to follow instructions and perform simple tasks are very important skills for work in this field.

HISTORY

In the early 20th century, as motion pictures were first developing, the roles of director and producer were combined in one person. European filmmakers such as Georges Melies and Leon Gaumont and New Yorker Edwin S. Porter directed, filmed, and produced very short movies. The first woman to become a director and producer was Alice Guy, who started the Solax Company in New York in 1910. The film industry settled in Hollywood and began to consolidate in the first two decades of the 20th century, as jobs were differentiated. Major studios assembled large staffs, so all stages of production from conception to financing and directing could be performed within a single studio. Twentieth Century Fox, for example, would have producers, writers, directors, and actors on staff to choose from for each film. Small producers were forced out of business as major studios grew to have a monopoly on the industry.

Learn More About It

Apel, Melanie Ann. *Cool Careers Without College for Film and Television Buffs.* New York: Rosen Publishing Group, 2008.

Dzyak, Brian. *What I Really Want to Do on Set in Hollywood: A Guide to Real Jobs in the Film Industry.* Los Angeles: Lone Eagle Publishing Company, 2008.

Ebert, Roger, and David Bordwell. *Awake in the Dark: The Best of Roger Ebert.* Chicago: University of Chicago Press, 2008.

Gregory, Georgina, Ros Healy, and Ewa Mazierksa. *Careers in Media and Film: The Essential Guide.* Thousand Oaks, Calif.: Sage Publications Ltd., 2008.

The New York Times. The New York Times Guide to the Best 1,000 Movies Ever Made. Rev. ed. New York: St. Martin's Griffin, 2004.

Thompson, Kristin, and David Bordwell. *Film History: An Introduction.* 3d ed. New York: McGraw-Hill Humanities/Social Sciences/Languages, 2009.

In the 1950s the dominance of major studios in film production was curbed by an antitrust court decision, and more independent producers were able to find projects. Changes in the United States tax code made independent producing more profitable. At the same time, the growth of television provided new opportunities for producers, not only for television films, but news programs, weekly entertainment programs, sports broadcasts, talk shows, and documentaries. More recently, the video industry, particularly in the areas of music and education, has opened up even more production jobs.

The industry is becoming increasingly international; many foreign-made films and videos are now financed by Americans, and a number of American motion picture companies are under foreign ownership. Currently many producers work on a project-by-project basis. Independent producers must be good salespersons to market a project to a television or movie studio and to other financial backers. They will try to involve popular actors and media personalities with the project from its inception in order to attract a studio's interest. Studios hire production assistants to facilitate the work of the producer and other staff members.

THE JOB

The work of a production assistant is not glamorous, but production is the best place to learn about the film and television industries. All hiring, casting, and decision making is done by members of production; they are involved with a project from the very beginning through its final stages. The producer is in charge—he or she is responsible for coordinating the activities of all employees involved in a production. Producers oversee the budget, and they have the final word on most decisions made for a film or television show.

The responsibilities of PAs range from making sure the star has coffee in the morning to stopping street traffic so a director can film a scene. They photocopy the script for actors, assist in setting up equipment, and perform other menial tasks. The best PAs know where to be at the right time to make themselves useful. Production can be stressful; time is money and mistakes can be very costly. Assistants must be prepared to handle unforeseen problems, smooth out difficulties, and help out as quickly as possible.

Duties may include keeping production files in order. These files will include contracts, budgets, page changes (old pages from a script that has been revised), and other records. The documents must be kept organized and accessible for whenever the producer may need them.

Production assistants may also have to keep the producer's production folder in order and up-to-date. The production folder contains everything the producer needs to know about the production at a glance. It is particularly useful for times when a producer is on location away from the studio and cannot access the office files. PAs make sure that the folder includes the shooting schedule, the most recent version of the budget, cast and crew lists with phone numbers, a phone sheet detailing all production-related phone calls the producer needs to make, and the up-to-date shooting script. As new versions of these forms are created, PAs update the producer's folder and file the older versions for reference. This information may also be maintained in a computer database.

PAs may also be in charge of making sure that the producer gets the dailies, the film shot each day. They schedule an hour or so in a producer's schedule to watch the dailies and to make related calls to discuss them with other staff members.

PAs perform a number of other administrative and organizational tasks. They make travel reservations, arrange hotel accommodations, and arrange for rehearsal space. They run errands and communicate messages for producers, directors, actors, musicians, and other members of the technical crew.

Production assistant is the lowest position on the film or television crew. It is an entry-level job that gives someone interested in film and broadcast media the experience and contacts to move into other areas of the industry. PAs often get stuck with undesirable tasks like sweeping floors, guarding sets, or finding a particular brand of green tea for a demanding diva. However, a film, television, or video production would not happen without production assistants on the set or in the studio.

REQUIREMENTS

High School

To work in the film or television industry, you should have an understanding of the artistic and technical aspects of production, as well as a broad knowledge of the industry itself. Take courses in photography, broadcast journalism, and media to learn about cameras and sound equipment. Take classes in art and art history to learn about visual composition, and English to develop communication skills. Business and accounting courses can help you prepare for the bookkeeping requirements of office work.

Postsecondary Training

There are no formal education requirements for production assistants. Most people in the industry consider the position a stepping-stone into other careers in the industry. You'll learn much of what you'll need to know on the set of a film, following the instructions of crew members and other assistants. Though a film school education can't guarantee entry into the business, it can give you an understanding of the industry and help you make some connections. Many film students work part time or on a contract basis as production assistants to gain experience while they are still in school. In the United States there are more than 1,000 colleges, universities, and trade schools that offer classes in film or television studies; more than 120 of these offer undergraduate programs, and more than 50 grant master's degrees. A small number of Ph.D. programs also exist. According to the American Film Institute, the most reputable are Columbia University in New York, New York University, the University of California at Los Angeles, and the University of Southern California. You may choose to major in English or theater as an undergraduate, then apply to graduate film schools. There are many good undergraduate programs in film and video with concentrations in such areas as directing, acting, editing, producing, screenwriting, cinematography, broadcast engineering, and television. Some people break into the business without formal training by volunteering on as many film productions as they can, getting to know professionals in the business, and making valuable connections in the industry. Your chances of moving up, however, are better if you have a college degree.

Other Requirements

To be a successful production assistant, you need an agreeable personality and you must be willing to follow instructions and perform simple tasks. You need to catch on quickly to the things you're taught. Organizational skills will help you keep track of the many different aspects of a production. Great ambition and dedication are very important, as getting paying jobs on a production will require persistence. Also, you won't get a great deal of recognition for your hours of work, so you need a sense of purpose and an understanding that you are "paying your dues." A love of movies, video, and television and a fascination with the industry, particularly an interest in the technical aspects of filmmaking, will help you keep focused. Though you need an outgoing personality for making connections on a production, you should be capable of sitting quietly on the sidelines when not needed.

EXPLORING

There are many ways to gain experience with filmmaking. Some high schools have film clubs and classes in film or video. Experience in theater can also be useful. To learn more, you can work as a volunteer for a local theater or a low budget film project; these positions are often advertised in local trade publications. You may also be able to volunteer with your state's film commission, helping to solicit production companies to do their filming in the state.

Students interested in production work should read as much as possible about the film and television industry, starting at a school or public library. Trade journals can be very helpful as well; the two most prominent ones are *Daily Variety* (http://www.variety.com) and *The Hollywood Reporter* (http://www.hollywoodreporter.com). These resources will have information about production studios that will prove very useful for prospective PAs. If you are interested in video production, read *Studio Monthly* (http://www.studiodaily.com/studiomonthly).

EMPLOYERS

Production assistants are hired by film and video production companies for individual projects. Some assistants are employed full time in the main offices of a production company or as personal assistants to producers or executives. Production assistants can also find full-time employment at television studios.

STARTING OUT

Look for internships, which may offer course credit if they are unpaid, by reading trade journals and contacting film and television studios. You can also find production opportunities listed on the Internet or through your state's film commission. To gain experience, you may have to work for free on some of your first productions to make contacts within the industry. Since this is an entry-level position, opportunities will open as other assistants advance.

ADVANCEMENT

Production assistant positions are usually considered temporary. After one or two years, production assistants have enough experience to move into other jobs, and there are numerous choices, depending on their interests. They may wish to go into editing, camera operation, lighting, sound, writing, directing, producing, or performing. All of these areas have a hierarchy of positions that allow a production assistant to work his or her way up to the top jobs. A production assistant can, for example, become a *line producer,* who works closely with the producer, signing checks, advising on union rules, and negotiating deals with studio personnel. An associate producer performs similar work. To become a producer or director requires years of experience and hard work.

EARNINGS

Because working as a production assistant is the starting point for most professionals and artists in the film industry, many people volunteer their time until they make connections and move into paid positions. Those assistants who can negotiate payment may make between $200 and $400 a week, but they may only have the opportunity to work on a few projects a year. Production assistants working full time in an office may start at around $20,000 a year, but with experience can make around $65,000. Full-time production assistants may belong to the Office and Professional Employees International Union, which negotiates salaries. Experienced script supervisors, production office coordinators, and continuity coordinators have the opportunity to join Local #161 of the International Alliance of Theatrical Stage Employees, Moving Picture Technicians, Artists and Allied Crafts of the United States, Its Territories, and Canada. Its members may earn more than $180 a day when working for a production company.

According to Salary.com, production assistants earned a median annual salary of $27,455 in 2011. Salaries ranged from less than $25,272 to $29,730 or more annually.

Those working on a project-to-project basis won't receive any fringe benefits, but those employed full-time with a production company can expect health coverage and retirement benefits.

WORK ENVIRONMENT

A film set is an exciting environment, but the production assistant may be treated poorly there. With a positive attitude, energy, and a desire to be useful, PAs will earn respect from the production department.

There are unwritten rules that should be followed. A production assistant who works for the producer or for the studio can be seen as an outsider in the eyes of the director and the creative team, so PAs should be respectful and well behaved. This means that production assistants should be quiet, stay out of the way, and avoid touching sets and equipment. If a production assistant behaves as a guest, but remains helpful when needed, he or she will earn a good reputation that will be valuable for his or her career advancement.

The work environment will vary; PAs may be required on location, or may work mainly in the studio. Production assistants must be willing to work long, demanding hours. Film productions are typically off schedule and over budget, requiring dedication from all those involved. Production assistants and other crew members often go days without seeing family members.

OUTLOOK

There will always be a need for assistants in film and television production. However, since it is such a good entry-level position for someone who wants to make connections and learn about the industry, competition for jobs can be tough. Fortunately, production assistants usually do not stay in their jobs more than one or two years, so turnover is fairly frequent. PAs will find employment anywhere a motion picture, television show, or video is being filmed, but significant opportunities exist in Los Angeles and New York—the production hubs of the industry. There may be opportunities at local television stations or smaller production companies that produce educational and corporate videos.

FOR MORE INFORMATION

For information about colleges with film and television programs of study, and to read interviews with filmmakers, visit the AFI Web site.
American Film Institute (AFI)
2021 North Western Avenue
Los Angeles, CA 90027-1657
Tel: 323-856-7600
E-mail: information@afi.com
http://www.afi.com

The ASC Web site has articles from American Cinematographer *magazine, industry news, and a tips and tricks for cinematographers section.*
American Society of Cinematographers (ASC)
PO Box 2230
Hollywood, CA 90078-2230
Tel: 800-448-0145
http://www.theasc.com

For information about careers in cable TV, contact
National Cable and Telecommunications Association
25 Massachusetts Avenue, NW, Suite 100
Washington, DC 20001-1434
Tel: 202-222-2300
http://www.ncta.com

Visit the FAQ section of the PGA Web site to read about producer careers.
Producers Guild of America (PGA)
8530 Wilshire Boulevard, Suite 450
Beverly Hills, CA 90211-3115
Tel: 310-358-9020
E-mail: info@producersguild.org
http://www.producersguild.org

Production Designers and Art Directors

OVERVIEW

In films, videos, and television commercials, *production designers* are responsible for the overall look of the visual elements and approve the props, costumes, and locations. *Art directors* are the top assistants of production designers; they ensure that the production designer's vision is implemented. In the past, the art director title was used to denote the head of the art department. The Academy Award for Best Art Direction still references art directors, but the award is actually given to top production designers.

HISTORY

In the early days of the motion picture industry, directors were usually responsible for creating the "look" of their films. But as filmmaking became more complex and more movies were made, directors began to rely on skilled artists to handle the visual aspects of their films.

Production designers and art directors did not receive much credit for their important work shaping the visual elements of films until 1939, according to the Art Directors Guild & Scenic, Title, and Graphic Artists. According to its Web site, famed producer David O. Selznick "agreed to give the new credit of production designer to William Cameron Menzies for his brilliant work on the classic film" *Gone With the Wind*. Menzies' storyboards and illustrations are credited with revolutionizing the industry and showing the important role production designers play in the filmmaking process. Production designers and art directors first began meeting informally in Los Angeles in 1924. This

QUICK FACTS

School Subjects
Art
Computer science
Theater/dance

Personal Skills
Artistic
Communication/ideas

Work Environment
Indoors and outdoors
Primarily multiple locations

Minimum Education Level
Bachelor's degree

Salary Range
$41,670 to $110,470 to
 $160,060+

Certification or Licensing
None available

Outlook
About as fast as the average

DOT
164

GOE
01.01.01

NOC
5131

O*NET-SOC
27–1011.00

gathering eventually became the Art Directors Guild & Scenic, Title, and Graphic Artists. Today, it has a membership of about 2,000. United Scenic Artists Local USA 829 is another member organization for production designers and art directors and a variety of other arts-related professionals.

THE JOB

Production designers are responsible for all visual aspects of on-screen productions. In film and video and broadcast advertising, the production designer has a wide variety of responsibilities and often interacts with an enormous number of creative professionals. Working with directors, producers, and other professionals, production designers interpret scripts and create or select settings in order to visually convey the story or the message. The production designer oversees and channels the talents of set decorators and designers, model makers, location managers, propmasters, construction coordinators, and special and visual effects people. In addition, production designers work with writers, unit production managers, cinematographers, costume designers, and post-production staff, including editors and employees responsible for scoring and titles. The production designer is ultimately responsible for all visual aspects of the finished product.

The production designer has to consider many things when designing the look of a movie. They need to incorporate the director's vision for the film, the actual story outlined in the screenplay, and the budget that is available to spend on props, costumes, sets, and other elements that help set the visual mood of a film. If a movie is to be shot on location, the production designer travels to potential sites to determine if they will be appropriate for use. They may also work with *location scouts,* who do the leg work to find just the right setting for particular scenes.

Once a production designer gathers all of this information, he or she creates sketches or models (or uses a computer software program to do so) that illustrate their vision for the visual elements of the film for the producer, director, cinematographer, and other departments. A concept artist or illustrator is sometimes hired to prepare these presentations. After the sketches and/or models are approved, the production designer works with the production manager and line producer to finalize a budget for the art department so that construction on the sets can begin. They also work with set designers to prepare drawings that can be used by the construction coordinator.

Preproduction on a film is designed to be the most efficient use of time and money. The time budgeted for set design and construction is tight and with a set deadline there is constant revision and planning to complete the sets on time for the scenic painters and decorators to complete their contributions and have them ready for shooting.

Because each film is different, and often it has a group of filmmakers that have not worked together before, things do not always work out as planned. It is to the credit of film professionals that they are able to adapt and compensate to make the impossible possible.

Production designers supervise the project from preproduction through production with the assistance of *art directors*. Art directors are the top assistants of production designers. They must have both creative and management skills to ensure that the production designer's vision is properly implemented. They are responsible for the entire operation of the production division or just particular departments such as construction, props, locations, special effects, and set dressing.

REQUIREMENTS
High School
There are a variety of high school courses that will provide both a taste of college-level offerings and an idea of the skills necessary for success on the job. These courses include art, drawing, art history, graphic design, illustration, theater, photography, advertising, shop, animation, and desktop publishing.

Other useful courses that you should take in high school include business, drama, English, technical drawing, cultural studies, psychology, and social science. Finally, take as many computer science courses as possible. Because of the rapidly increasing use of computers in design work, it is essential to have a thorough understanding of how computer-aided design programs work. For small-budget films, the production designer or art director may be responsible for using these software programs; for bigger budget movies, a staff person, under the direction of the designer or director, may use these programs.

Postsecondary Training
Many production designers and art directors attend film school and earn degrees in film studies, film production, or related fields. Others earn traditional degrees in theater, history, literature, or design. In addition to course work at the college level, many universities and professional art schools offer graduates or students in their final

year a variety of workshop projects and internships. These programs provide students with opportunities to develop their personal design styles as well as their portfolios.

Other Requirements
The work of production designers and art directors requires creativity, imagination, curiosity, and a sense of adventure. Art directors must be able to work with all sorts of specialized equipment and computer software, such as computer-aided design programs, as well as make presentations on the ideas behind their work.

The ability to work well with different people is a must for production designers and art directors. They must always be up-to-date on new techniques, trends, and attitudes. And because deadlines are a constant part of the work, an ability to handle stress and pressure well is key. Time-management skills are also important.

EXPLORING

Developing your own artistic talent is one good way to explore your interest in the field of production design, and this can be accomplished through self-training (reading books and practicing); through courses in painting, drawing, computer-aided design, or other creative arts; or by working with a group of friends to create a movie. At the very least, you should develop your "creative eye," that is, your ability to develop ideas visually. One way to do this is by familiarizing yourself with great works, such as highly creative motion pictures, television shows, videos, or commercials. You should also read books about production design. Here is one suggestion: *The Art Direction Handbook for Film,* by Michael Rizzo (St. Louis, Mo.: Focal Press, 2005). Finally, ask a teacher or school counselor to arrange an information interview with a production designer or art director.

EMPLOYERS

Typical employers include film and television production houses, movie studios, multimedia developers, computer games developers, and television stations. Other nonentertainment industry employers include advertising agencies, publishing houses, museums, packaging firms, photography studios, marketing and public relations firms, Web designers, desktop publishing outfits, digital prepress houses, or printing companies.

STARTING OUT

The positions of production designer and art director are not entry level. Typically, a person on a career track toward the position of production designer or art director is hired as an assistant to an established professional.

Serving as an intern is a good way to get experience and develop skills. Graduates should also consider taking an entry-level job at a film studio to gain initial experience.

ADVANCEMENT

Since they head the art department, many production designers are happy to continue working as designers throughout their careers. They can advance by seeking employment with larger production companies and better-known directors and producers. Some production designers start their own freelance businesses. A few become directors or producers.

Art directors advance by becoming production designers, by working on more prestigious film projects, and by seeking employment with larger companies.

EARNINGS

Mean annual earnings for art directors employed in the motion picture and video industries were $110,470 in 2009, according to the U.S. Department of Labor (DOL). Salaries for all art directors ranged from less than $41,670 to $160,060 or more.

The weekly base pay for a motion picture production designer who is a member of the International Alliance of Theatrical Stage Employees is approximately $3,000, but top production designers can negotiate higher salaries of more than $10,000 per week. Production designers who work on nonunion productions typically have lower earnings.

Film companies employing production designers and art directors pay into the Art Directors Guild's Health & Pension Fund. Production designers and art directors who are members of the International Alliance of Theatrical Stage Employees or National Association of Broadcast Employees and Technicians receive health insurance and a pension as part of their membership benefits. Freelance nonunion production designers and art directors employed in the motion picture and television industries are usually responsible for providing their own health insurance and other benefits.

WORK ENVIRONMENT

Production designers and art directors often work under pressure of a deadline and yet must remain calm and pleasant when dealing with coworkers. They must work as many hours as required—usually many more than 40 hours per week—in order to finish projects according to predetermined schedules. Some travel is required to scout potential locations for filming.

OUTLOOK

The DOL predicts that employment for production designers and art directors who work in the motion picture and video industries will grow about as fast as the average for all careers through 2018. These professionals play a major role in the look of a film and, as a result, will continue to be in steady demand in coming years. However, it is important to note that there are more production designers and art directors than the number of available job openings. As a result, those wishing to enter the field will encounter keen competition for salaried, staff positions as well as for freelance work.

FOR MORE INFORMATION

For industry information, contact
Art Directors Club
106 West 29th Street
New York, NY 10001-5301
Tel: 212-643-1440
E-mail: info@adcglobal.org
http://www.adcglobal.org

For information on art directors who are employed in the moving picture industry, contact
Art Directors Guild & Scenic, Title, and Graphic Artists
11969 Ventura Boulevard, 2nd Floor
Studio City, CA 91604-2630
Tel: 818-762-9995
http://www.adg.org

This union represents production designers, art directors, and other film industry professionals working in film, television, industrial shows, theater, opera, ballet, commercials, and exhibitions. Visit its Web site for more information.

United Scenic Artists Local 829
29 West 38th Street, 15th Floor
New York, NY 10018-5504
Tel: 212-581-0300
http://www.usa829.org

INTERVIEW

Professor Annette Insdorf is the director of undergraduate film studies at Columbia University in New York City. She discussed the program with the editors of Careers in Focus: Film.

Q. Can you please tell us about Columbia's undergraduate film major and your professional background?

A. Columbia's undergraduate film major is scholarly rather than production-oriented. We believe that learning the technical aspects of filmmaking—how to shoot and edit—is simple; it's harder to have a story worth telling. Our courses are anchored in film history, and we encourage an interdisciplinary approach. A student with a solid liberal arts education has a better sense of his or her place in the world, and of how films express a variety of eras as well as nations.

   In terms of my own background, I did my Ph.D. at Yale University in literature, and immediately began teaching film history and criticism.

Q. Your program Web site mentions that the program is writing intensive. Can you detail how writing is integrated into students' education?

A. The film studies major at Columbia is similar to what the English major was to my own generation—the study of a rich narrative art form, leading to the mastery of expressing yourself with clarity as well as elegance. Students write papers in almost all our classes, honing their critical ability at the same time that they develop creative skill in our screenwriting workshops.

Q. What is one thing that young people may not know about a career in film?

A. Some of the most wonderful motion picture careers are not necessarily directing ones. Many of our students have found gratifying work in a number of other areas, including producing;

distribution; publicity; programming (museums, film festivals, etc.); and teaching.

Q. What types of students pursue study in your program? What are their typical career goals?

A. It's hard to generalize, as we have approximately 75 under-graduate film majors at any given time, and their interests are varied. The only qualities they share might be a passion for movies and a diligent work ethic.

Q. What advice would you offer film studies majors as they graduate and look for jobs?

A. If your financial situation permits, it's sometimes better to take an unpaid internship with a film company, as it can lead to a paid position.

Q. What does the future hold for your program?

A. We are delighted to be continuing on our path of excellence: we hope to keep offering a blend of stimulating courses in film history, theory, criticism, and production, with alumni like Ramin Bahrani and Anna Boden.

Public Relations Specialists

OVERVIEW

Public relations (PR) specialists develop and maintain programs that present a favorable public image for an individual or organization. They provide information to the target audience (generally, the public at large) about the client, its goals and accomplishments, and any further plans or projects that may be of public interest.

PR specialists may be employed by corporations, government agencies, nonprofit organizations—almost any type of organization. Many PR specialists hold positions in public relations consulting firms or work for advertising agencies. There are approximately 275,200 public relations specialists in the United States. Only a small percentage of this number work in the movie industry.

HISTORY

The first public relations counsel was a reporter named Ivy Ledbetter Lee, who in 1906 was named press representative for coal mine operators. Labor disputes were becoming a large concern of the operators, and they had run into problems because of their continual refusal to talk to the press and the hired miners. Lee convinced the mine operators to start responding to press questions and supply the press with information on the mine activities.

During and after World War II, the rapid advancement of communications techniques prompted firms to realize they needed professional help to ensure their messages were given proper public attention. Manufacturing firms that had turned their production facilities over to the war effort returned to the manufacture of peacetime products and enlisted the aid of public relations professionals to forcefully bring products and the company name before the buying public.

Large business firms, labor unions, and service organizations, such as the American Red Cross, Boy Scouts of America, and the YMCA, began to recognize the value of establishing positive, healthy relationships with the public that they served and depended on for support. The need for effective public relations was often emphasized when circumstances beyond a company's or institution's control created unfavorable reaction from the public.

Public relations specialists also play a significant role in the motion picture industry. They present upbeat information about film professionals and movie studios to the public in order to create a positive buzz and encourage people to watch movies. They also provide important damage control when actors and other film professionals become embroiled in scandals that may affect their careers and popularity at the box office.

THE JOB

Public relations specialists are employed to do a variety of tasks. They may be employed primarily as writers, creating reports, news releases, and booklet texts. Others write speeches or create copy for

On the Web

Academy of Motion Picture Arts and Sciences
http://www.oscars.org

AMC Filmsite
http://www.filmsite.org

Box Office Mojo
http://www.boxofficemojo.com

FilmFestivals.com
http://www.filmfestivals.com

The Internet Movie Database
http://www.imdb.com

RogerEbert.com
http://rogerebert.suntimes.com

The Walt Disney Family Museum
http://disney.go.com/disneyatoz/familymuseum

radio, TV, Web sites, or film sequences. These workers often spend much of their time contacting the press, radio, and TV as well as magazines on behalf of the employer. Some PR specialists work more as editors than writers, fact-checking and rewriting employee publications, newsletters, shareholder reports, and other management communications. Specialists may choose to concentrate in graphic design, using their background knowledge of art and layout for developing brochures, booklets, and photographic communications. Other PR workers handle special events, such as press parties, award shows, convention exhibits, open houses, or anniversary celebrations.

Public relations specialists employed by movie studios and television networks are concerned with efforts that will promote interest and create a buzz about their employer's movies or television shows. They work closely with their organization's marketing department to promote new movies, arrange print and broadcast interviews with the movie's stars or director, and undertake any other method of publicity that will encourage people to watch the movie or television show.

Many PR workers act as consultants (rather than staff) of a company (such as a movie studio or an independent production company), association, college, hospital, or other institution. These workers have the advantage of being able to operate independently, state opinions objectively, and work with more than one type of business or association.

PR specialists are called upon to work with the public opinion aspects of almost every corporate or institutional problem. In terms of the motion picture industry, this might include putting the best possible "spin" on an actor's controversial or unlawful behavior (such as a nightclub fight with paparazzi, a substance abuse problem, or offensive comments that the actor thought he or she was making off the record), explaining a studio's bargaining position during a strike by cinematographers, or detailing a production company's efforts to be environmentally friendly during filming in a pristine national park.

REQUIREMENTS

High School

While in high school, take courses in English, journalism, public speaking, humanities, and languages because public relations is based on effective communication with others. These courses will help you develop your skills in written and oral communication as well as provide a better understanding of different fields and industries to be publicized.

Postsecondary Training
Most people employed in public relations have a college degree. Major fields of study most beneficial to developing the proper skills are public relations, English, and journalism. Some employers feel that majoring in the area in which the public relations person will eventually work is the best training. For example, if you are interested in working in the film or television industries, you might consider majoring in film or broadcasting. Knowledge of business administration is most helpful, as is an innate talent for selling. A graduate degree may be required for managerial positions. People with a bachelor's degree in public relations can find staff positions with either an organization or a public relations firm.

More than 200 colleges and about 100 graduate schools offer degree programs in public relations. In addition, many other colleges offer at least courses in the field. Public relations programs are sometimes administered by the journalism or communication departments of schools. In addition to courses in theory and techniques of public relations, interested individuals may study organization, management and administration, and practical applications and often specialize in areas such as business, government, and nonprofit organizations. Other preparation includes courses in creative writing, psychology, communications, advertising, and journalism.

Certification or Licensing
The Public Relations Society of America and the International Association of Business Communicators accredit public relations workers who have at least five years of experience in the field and pass a comprehensive examination. Such accreditation is a sign of competence in this field, although it is not a requirement for employment.

Other Requirements
Today's public relations specialist must be a businessperson first, both to understand how to perform successfully in business and to comprehend the needs and goals of the organization or client. Additionally, the public relations specialist needs to be a strong writer and speaker, with good interpersonal, leadership, and organizational skills. PR specialists who work in the motion picture industry should be familiar with how the industry works, its major players, and key issues and trends in the field.

EXPLORING

Almost any experience in working with other people will help you to develop strong interpersonal skills, which are crucial in public relations. The possibilities are almost endless. Summer work on a newspaper or trade paper or with a television station or film company may give insight into communications media. Working as a volunteer on a political campaign can help you to understand the ways in which people can be persuaded. Being selected as a page for the U.S. Congress or a state legislature will help you grasp the fundamentals of government processes. A job in retail will help you to understand some of the principles of product presentation. A teaching job will develop your organization and presentation skills. These are just some of the jobs that will let you explore areas of public relations. Another way to learn more about the field is by talking with a PR specialist about his or her career. Ask a teacher for help arranging such an interview.

EMPLOYERS

Public relations specialists hold about 275,200 jobs. Only a small percentage of this number are employed in the film industry. Workers may be paid employees of the organization they represent or they may be part of a public relations firm that works for organizations on a contract basis. Others are involved in fund-raising or political campaigning. Public relations may be done for a corporation, retail business, service company, utility, association, nonprofit organization, or educational institution.

Most PR firms are located in large cities that are centers of communications. New York, Chicago, San Francisco, Los Angeles, and Washington, D.C., are good places to start a search for a public relations job. The cities of Los Angeles and New York provide the best job prospects for aspiring film industry PR specialists. Nevertheless, there are many good opportunities in cities across the United States.

STARTING OUT

There is no clear-cut formula for getting a job in public relations. Individuals often enter the field after gaining preliminary experience in another occupation closely allied to the field, usually some segment of communications, and frequently, in journalism. Coming into public relations from newspaper work is still a recommended route. Another good method is to gain initial employment as a public relations trainee or intern, or as a clerk, secretary, or research assistant in a public relations department or a consulting firm.

ADVANCEMENT

In some large companies, an entry-level public relations specialist may start as a trainee in a formal training program for new employees. In others, new employees may expect to be assigned to work that has a minimum of responsibility. They may assemble clippings or do rewrites on material that has already been accepted. They may make posters or assist in conducting polls or surveys, or compile reports from data submitted by others.

As workers acquire experience, they are given more responsibility. They write news releases, direct polls or surveys, or advance to writing speeches for company officials. Progress may seem to be slow, because some skills take a long time to master.

Some advance in responsibility and salary in the same firm in which they started. Others find that the path to advancement is to accept a more attractive position in another firm.

The goal of many public relations specialists is to open an independent office or to join an established consulting firm. To start an independent office requires a large outlay of capital and an established reputation in the field. However, those who are successful in operating their own consulting firms probably attain the greatest financial success in the public relations field.

EARNINGS

Public relations specialists earned median annual salaries of $51,960 in 2009, according to the U.S. Department of Labor (DOL). Salaries ranged from less than $30,520 to more than $96,630.

Many PR workers receive a range of fringe benefits from corporations and agencies employing them, including bonus/incentive compensation, stock options, profit sharing/pension plans/401(k) programs, medical benefits, life insurance, financial planning, maternity/paternity leave, paid vacations, and family college tuition. Bonuses can range from 5 to 100 percent of base compensation and often are based on individual and/or company performance.

WORK ENVIRONMENT

Public relations specialists generally work in offices with adequate secretarial help, regular salary increases, and expense accounts.

They are expected to make a good appearance in tasteful, conservative clothing. They must have social poise, and their conduct in their personal life is important to their firms or their clients. The public relations specialist may have to entertain business associates.

The PR specialist seldom works the conventional office hours for many weeks at a time; although the workweek may consist of 35 to 40 hours, these hours may be supplemented by evenings and even weekends when meetings must be attended and other special events covered. Time behind the desk may represent only a small part of the total working schedule. Travel is often an important and necessary part of the job.

The life of the PR worker is so greatly determined by the job that many consider this a disadvantage. Because the work is concerned with public opinion, it is often difficult to measure the results of performance and to sell the worth of a public relations program to an employer or client. Competition in the consulting field is keen, and if a firm loses an account, some of its personnel may be affected. The demands it makes for anonymity will be considered by some as one of the profession's less inviting aspects. Public relations involves much more hard work and a great deal less glamour than is popularly supposed.

OUTLOOK

Employment of public relations professionals is expected to grow much faster than the average for all occupations through 2018, according to the DOL. Competition will be keen for beginning jobs in public relations because so many job seekers are enticed by the perceived glamour and appeal of the field; those with both education and experience will have an advantage.

Most large companies have some sort of public relations resource, either through their own staff or through the use of a firm of consultants. They are expected to expand their public relations activities and create many new jobs. More of the smaller companies are hiring public relations specialists, adding to the demand for these workers. Additionally, as a result of recent corporate scandals, more public relations specialists will be hired to help improve the images of companies and regain the trust of the public.

There will continue to be good opportunities for PR specialists in the movie and television industries. Presenting a positive public image is key to success for actors and studios. PR specialists help convey this image to the public, and provide damage control when potentially negative situations arise. The DOL predicts that employment for public relations managers who work in the motion picture and video industries will grow faster than the average for all careers through 2018.

FOR MORE INFORMATION

For industry information, contact
International Association of Business Communicators
601 Montgomery Street, Suite 1900
San Francisco, CA 94111-2623
Tel: 415-544-4700
http://www.iabc.com

For statistics, salary surveys, and other information about the profession, contact
Public Relations Society of America
33 Maiden Lane, 11th Floor
New York, NY 10038-5150
Tel: 212-460-1400
http://www.prsa.org

For information on program accreditation and professional development, contact
Canadian Public Relations Society
4195 Dundas Street West, Suite 346
Toronto, ON M8X 1Y4 Canada
Tel: 416-239-7034
E-mail: admin@cprs.ca
http://www.cprs.ca

Screenwriters

OVERVIEW

Screenwriters write scripts for movies, television shows, documentaries, and other productions. They may choose themes themselves, or they may write on a theme assigned by a producer or director, sometimes adapting plays or novels into screenplays. Screenwriting is an art, a craft, and a business. It is a career that requires imagination and creativity, the ability to tell a story using both dialogue and pictures, and the ability to negotiate with producers and studio executives.

HISTORY

In 1894, Thomas Edison invented the kinetograph to take a series of pictures of actions staged specifically for the camera. In October of the same year, the first film opened at Hoyt's Theatre in New York. It was a series of acts performed by such characters as a strongman, a contortionist, and trained animals. Even in these earliest motion pictures, the plot or sequence of actions the film would portray was written down before filming began.

Newspaperman Roy McCardell was the first person to be hired for the specific job of writing for motion pictures. He wrote captions for photographs in a weekly entertainment publication. When he was employed by Biograph to write 10 scenarios, or stories, at $10 apiece, it caused a flood of newspapermen to try their hand at screenwriting.

The early films, which ran only about a minute and were photographs of interesting movement, grew into story films, which ran between nine and 15 minutes. The demand for original plots led to the development of story departments at each of the motion picture companies in the period from 1910 to 1915. The story departments were responsible for writing the stories and also for reading and evaluating material that came from outside sources. Stories usually came from writers, but some were purchased from actors on the lot. The actor Genevieve (Gene) Gauntier was paid $20 per reel of film for her first scenarios.

There was a continuing need for scripts because usually a studio bought a story one month, filmed the next, and released the film the month after. Some of the most popular stories in these early films were Wild West tales and comedies.

Longer story films began to use titles, and as motion pictures became longer and more sophisticated, so did the titles. In 1909–10, there was an average of 80 feet of title per 1,000 feet of film. By 1926, the average increased to 250 feet of title per 1,000 feet. The titles included dialogue, description, and historical background.

In 1920, the first Screen Writers Guild was established to ensure fair treatment of writers, and in 1927, the Academy of Motion Picture Arts and Sciences was formed, including a branch for writers. The first sound film, *The Jazz Singer,* was also produced in 1927. Screenwriting changed dramatically to adapt to the new technology.

From the 1950s to the 1980s, the studios gradually declined, and more independent film companies and individuals were able to break into the motion picture industry. The television industry began to

Learn More About It

Cowgill, Linda J. *Writing Short Films: Structure and Content for Screenwriters.* 2d ed. Los Angeles: Lone Eagle Publishing Company, 2005.

Hamlett, Christina. *Screenwriting for Teens: The 100 Principles of Screenwriting Every Budding Writer Must Know.* Studio City, Calif.: Michael Wiese Productions, 2006.

Trottier, David. *The Screenwriter's Bible: A Complete Guide to Writing, Formatting, and Selling Your Script.* 4th ed. Los Angeles: Silman-James Press, 2005.

Vines, James. *Q&A: The Working Screenwriter: An In-the-Trenches Perspective of Writing Movies in Today's Film Industry.* Bloomington, Ind.: AuthorHouse, 2006.

Walter, Richard. *Essentials of Screenwriting: The Art, Craft, and Business of Film and Television Writing.* New York: Plume, 2010.

thrive in the 1950s, further increasing the number of opportunities for screenwriters. During the 1960s, people began to graduate from the first education programs developed specifically for screenwriting.

Today, most Americans have spent countless hours viewing films and programs on television and movie screens, as well as the Internet and mobile electronic devices. Familiarity with these mediums has led many writers to attempt writing screenplays. This has created an intensely fierce marketplace with many more screenplays being rejected than accepted each year.

THE JOB

Screenwriters write scripts for all types of movies—including dramas, comedies, adventures, westerns, documentaries, animated features, and training films. They may write original stories, or get inspiration from newspapers, magazines, books, or other sources. They may also write scripts for continuing television series and made-for-TV movies.

Motion picture screenwriters submit an original screenplay or adaptation of a book to a motion picture producer or studio. Scripts are written in a two-column format, one column for dialogue and sound, the other for video instructions. One page of script equals about one minute of running time, though it varies. Each page has about 150 words and takes about 20 seconds to read. Screenwriters send a query letter outlining their idea before they submit a script to a production company. Then they send a standard release form and wait at least a month for a response. Studios buy many more scripts than are actually produced, and studios often will buy a script only with provisions that the original writer or another writer will rewrite it to their specifications.

Screenwriters may work on a staff of writers and producers for a large company. Or they may work independently for smaller companies that hire only freelance production teams.

REQUIREMENTS

High School

You can develop your writing skills by taking English, theater, speech, and journalism classes. Belonging to a debate team can also help you learn how to express your ideas within a specific time allotment and framework. History, government, and foreign language can contribute to a well-rounded education, necessary for creating intelligent scripts. Taking business courses can be useful in understanding basic business principles you will encounter in the film industry.

Postsecondary Training

There are no set educational requirements for screenwriters. A college degree is desirable, especially a liberal arts education, which exposes you to a wide range of subjects. An undergraduate or graduate film program will likely include courses in screenwriting, film theory, and other subjects that will teach you about the film industry and its history. A creative writing program will involve you with workshops and seminars that will help you develop fiction-writing skills.

Many colleges and universities have film departments, but some of the most respected film schools are the University of California–Los Angeles (http://www.tft.ucla.edu/programs/ftvdm), the University of Southern California (http://roski.usc.edu/), the American Film Institute (http://www.afi.com), and Columbia University (http://arts

And the Oscar Goes To . . .

The following screenwriters have won the Oscar for best original screenplay in recent years:

2010: David Seidler for *The King's Speech*
2009: Mark Boal for *The Hurt Locker*
2008: Dustin Lance Black for *Milk*
2007: Diablo Cody for *Juno*
2006: Michael Arndt for *Little Miss Sunshine*
2005: Paul Haggis and Bobby Moresco for *Crash*
2004: Charlie Kaufman for *Eternal Sunshine of the Spotless Mind*
2003: Sofia Coppola for *Lost in Translation*
2002: Pedro Almodovar for *Talk to Her*
2001: Julian Fellowes for *Gosford Park*
2000: Cameron Crowe for *Almost Famous*
1999: Alan Ball for *American Beauty*
1998: Marc Norman and Tom Stoppard for *Shakespeare in Love*
1997: Matt Damon and Ben Affleck for *Good Will Hunting*
1996: Ethan Coen and Joel Coen for *Fargo*
1995: Christopher McQuarrie for *The Usual Suspects*
1994: Quentin Tarantino and Roger Avary for *Pulp Fiction*

For more films by Academy Award-winning screenwriters, visit http://awardsdatabase.oscars.org/ampas_awards/BasicSearchInput .jsp.

.columbia.edu/film). Contact these schools or visit their Web pages for information about course work and faculty.

Other Requirements

As a screenwriter, you must be able to create believable characters and develop a story. You must have technical skills, such as dialogue writing, creating plots, and doing research. In addition to creativity and originality, you also need an understanding of the marketplace for your work. You should be aware of what kinds of scripts are in demand by producers. Word processing skills are also helpful.

EXPLORING

One of the best ways to learn about screenwriting is to read and study scripts. It is advisable to watch a motion picture while simultaneously following the script. The scripts for such classic films as *Casablanca, Network,* and *Chinatown* are often taught in college screenwriting courses. You should read film-industry publications, such as *Daily Variety* (http://www.variety.com), *The Hollywood Reporter* (http://www.hollywoodreporter.com), and *Hollywood Scriptwriter* (http://www.hollywoodscriptwriter.com). There are many books about screenwriting, as well as computer software programs that assist with screenplay formatting.

The Sundance Institute, a nonprofit organization founded by the actor Robert Redford, offers a variety of programs and activities for aspiring screenwriters, including a five-day writing workshop, a screenplay reading series, and, most notably, an annual film festival. (For contact information, see the end of this article.)

Most states offer grants for emerging and established screenwriters and other artists. Contact your state's art council for guidelines and application materials. In addition, several arts groups and associations hold annual contests for screenwriters. To find out more about screenwriting contests, consult a reference work such as *The Writer's Market* (http://www.writersmarket.com).

Students may try to get their work performed locally. A teacher may be able to help you submit your work to a local radio or television station or to a publisher of plays.

EMPLOYERS

Most screenwriters work on a freelance basis, contracting with film and television production companies for individual projects.

STARTING OUT

The first step to getting a screenplay produced is to write a letter to the script editor of a production company describing yourself, your training, and your work. Ask if the editors would be interested in reading one of your scripts. If you receive an invitation to submit more, you'll then prepare a synopsis, or treatment, of the screenplay, which is usually from one to 10 pages. It should be in the form of a narrative short story, with little or no dialogue.

You should also pursue a manager or agent by sending along a brief letter describing a project you're working on. A list of agents is available from the Writers Guild of America (WGA). Whether you are a beginning or experienced screenwriter, it is best to have an agent, since studios, producers, and stars often return unsolicited manuscripts unopened to protect themselves from plagiarism charges. Agents provide access to studios and producers, interpret contracts, and negotiate deals.

It is wise to register your script (online registration is $10 for members, $22 for nonmembers, and $17 for students) with the WGA. Although registration offers no legal protection, it is proof that on a specific date you came up with a particular idea, treatment, or script. You should also keep a detailed journal that lists the contacts you've made, including the people who have read your script.

ADVANCEMENT

Competition is stiff among screenwriters, and a beginner will find it difficult to break into the field. More opportunities become available as a screenwriter gains experience and a reputation, but that is a process that can take many years. Rejection is a common occurrence in the field of screenwriting. Most successful screenwriters have had to send their screenplays to numerous production companies before they find one that likes their work.

Once they have sold some scripts, screenwriters may be able to join the WGA. Membership with the WGA guarantees the screenwriter a minimum wage for a production and other benefits such as arbitration. Some screenwriters, however, writing for minor productions, can have regular work and successful careers without WGA membership.

Those screenwriters who manage to break into the business can benefit greatly from recognition in the industry. In addition to creating their own scripts, some writers are also hired to "doctor" the scripts of others, using their expertise to revise scripts for production.

If a film proves very successful, a screenwriter will be able to command higher payment, and will be able to work on high-profile productions. Some of the most talented film screenwriters receive awards from the industry, most notably the Academy Award for best original or adapted screenplay.

EARNINGS

With some film stars making more than $10 million dollars a movie, many aspiring writers are under the misconception that film industry holds big paychecks for them as well. But film writers get paid a mere fraction of the salaries of on-screen talent. Typically, a writer will earn a percentage (approximately 1 percent) of the film's budget. Obviously, a lower budget film pays considerably less than a big production, starting at $15,000 or less. According to the WGA 2008 Theatrical and Television Basic Agreement, earnings for writers of an original screenplay ranged from $62,642 to $117,602 during the 2010–11 segment of the contract. The U.S. Department of Labor reports that writers employed in the motion picture and video industries had mean annual earnings of $85,420 in 2009.

Screenwriters who are WGA members are eligible to receive health benefits.

WORK ENVIRONMENT

Screenwriters who choose to freelance have the freedom to write when and where they choose. They must be persistent and patient; only one in 20 to 30 purchased or optioned screenplays is produced.

Screenwriters who work on the staff of a large company, for a television series, or under contract to a motion picture company may share writing duties with others.

Screenwriters who do not live in Hollywood or New York will likely have to travel to attend script conferences. They may even have to relocate for several weeks while a project is in production. Busy periods before and during film production are followed by long periods of inactivity and solitude. This forces many screenwriters, especially those just getting started in the field, to work other jobs and pursue other careers while they develop their talent and craft.

OUTLOOK

There is intense competition in the motion picture and television industries. As the movie industry grows, cable television expands, and digital technology allows for more programming, new opportunities will emerge. Television networks continue to need new material and new episodes for long-running series, as well as made-for-TV movies. Movie studios are always looking for new angles on action, adventure, horror, and comedy, especially romantic comedy stories. The demand for new screenplays should increase slightly in the next decade, but the number of screenwriters is growing at a faster rate. Outside the film and television industries, writers will continue to find opportunities in advertising agencies and educational and training video production houses.

FOR MORE INFORMATION

For guidelines on submitting a script for consideration for the Sundance Institute's screenwriting program, send a self-addressed stamped envelope to the institute or visit the following Web site:
Sundance Institute
8530 Wilshire Boulevard, 3rd Floor
Beverly Hills, CA 90211-3114
Tel: 310-360-1981
E-mail: institute@sundance.org
http://www.sundance.org

To learn more about the film industry, to read interviews and articles by noted screenwriters, and to find links to many other screenwriting-related sites on the Internet, visit the Web sites of the WGA.
Writers Guild of America (WGA)
East Chapter
250 Hudson Street
New York, NY 10013-1413
Tel: 212-767-7800
http://www.wgaeast.org

Writers Guild of America (WGA)
West Chapter
7000 West Third Street
Los Angeles, CA 90048-4329
Tel: 800-548-4532
http://www.wga.org

Visit the following Web site to read useful articles on screenwriting:
Screenwriter's Utopia
http://www.screenwritersutopia.com

INTERVIEW

Richard Walter is the chairman of the graduate program in screenwriting at the University of California–Los Angeles. He is also a screenwriter and the author of several books, including Essentials of Screenwriting: The Art, Craft, and Business of Film and Television Writing. *(Visit http://www.richardwalter.com to learn more about his career.) Richard discussed his program and the field of screenwriting with the editors of* Careers in Focus: Film.

Q. Can you please provide a brief overview of your program?

A. We offer a master of fine arts in screenwriting. Our orientation is dreadfully, wretchedly classical, that is, we embrace Aristotle's *Poetics* as the operator's manual for creators of dramatic narratives. We are story hard-liners, that is, we believe that everything else—character, dialogue, theme, setting, etc.—derives from story. We're a two-year program though many, perhaps most students, remain for a third year.

We operate on the academic quarter system: three 10-week quarters instead of the usual two 15-week semesters. This works very well for screenwriters. We are very much conservatory-oriented. Analysis and intellectual issues are left to our colleagues in cinema/media studies. All our writing courses are hands-on, practical writing workshops. Our signature course is an eight-credit graduate workshop with only eight writers around the table. Every student has to write a professional-quality, feature-length screenplay in each of the many sections offered every quarter. It meets once weekly for three hours, but there are also tutorial meetings with the instructor.

In their first quarter, our students endure a weekly one-hour lecture in which we explain and extol the essential principles we believe account for our students' success in making the transition from the academic to the professional arena (three best-screenplay Oscar nominations in the past three years; two Oscars in the same period; 10 major projects directed and/or produced by Steven Spielberg; etc.). In the second quarter, students hit the ground writing. They enroll in the feature screenplay workshop at least three times; ambitious students take it six or seven or more times. They end up not with a single showcase script but a body of work that includes a few scripts just to throw away. We provide a safe place for writers to reach and stretch and take risks and feel that they can fall on their faces and pick themselves up. We provide a community in which writers can struggle to find their own unique voice.

Q. What is one thing that young people may not know about a career in screenwriting?

A. Young people can't easily realize how difficult it is to make up a story that sustains the interest of an audience for a hundred minutes or a couple of hours. They place too much emphasis on talent and not enough on discipline, patience, and stamina. They don't understand that once you are established as a successful writer you have to keep plugging away writing speculative scripts or you may suddenly come to resemble old news and bad luck. They don't understand that writing never gets easy. The newcomer and the experienced professional alike suffer and struggle and endure. Young people place too much emphasis on directing and directors when, in fact, the first artist in film is not the director but the writer because she is just that: first. There is no purpose for fancy lenses and glitzy actors and slick scores and sexy cinematography if there isn't an engaging sequence of events, that is, a story, populated by characters worth caring about.

Q. What advice would you offer screenwriting majors as they graduate and look for jobs?

A. The writer's day job is her friend. It keeps writers solvent and sane, two closely related qualities. More importantly, it keeps writers in touch with the source of their drama: the humanity around them. The writer's dream to be successful enough to work in an isolated cabin in the woods or cottage at the beach is just that: a dream or, more precisely, a nightmare.

The key to success is to continue mix it up in society and to self-generate material, not waiting around for commissioned assignments or sales of previously written scripts. They should know that no credits constitute a writer's best credit. Exactly as movies romanticize and idealize the human condition, so also does the movie business. Agents and producers can project upon an inexperienced writer the idealized, romanticized notion of what they want her to be. They can't do this after the writer has had some development deals that did not develop or pictures that got made but bombed. This is the only business where inexperience trumps experience. In Hollywood, you start at the top and work your way down.

Q. What are the elements of a well-written screenplay?

A. Story, story, story. Character and dialogue are important, of course, but they have no meaning, no substance, outside the context of what they do and say, that is, the story. Characters do not have to be likeable. Some of the greatest protagonists are murderers and monsters—Oedipus, Medea, Macbeth, Richard III, Tony Soprano, Michael Corleone, J. R. Ewing. They need merely to be human. We need to feel not isolated but connected to them. Dialogue has to be peppy and perky and punchy and provocative, and those are just the p's! Dialogue has to be worth hearing all for itself, but it cannot be all for itself. It needs at the same time perpetually to advance story and character. This is no mean feat. It's why they pay writers so well when they pay us at all. A well-written screenplay is integrated—there is not a sight or sound that does not palpably, identifiably, measurably move the story forward. If a writer succeeds in keeping to this principle, it does not matter what the script is about, nor what happens in any particular scene. Readers and audience will be engaged.

Q. What do you like most and least about being a screenwriter?

A. I love the freedom of being (for the most part) my own boss and having the god-like experience of creating the universe of my script. There's a lot of power there. You want it to rain? It rains. Weary of the rain and you want the sun to shine? The sun shines. You want to kill someone—and who hasn't wanted to kill someone, however briefly, at one time or another? You can kill someone. Feel remorse? You can bring 'em back to life. How cool is that? Ultimately, though, screenwriters get paid for what others get scolded: day-dreaming. What beats trafficking in your own imagination and swapping your dreams for dollars?

The downside is the dread and the despair and disappointment and disillusion and depression, and those are just the d's! Drama is about feeling, and dramatists have to be people whose feelings are intense. We're talking about passionate souls here. And the ability to feel is the ability, of course, to experience elation but also the opposite of that: pain. I'm privileged to have met zillions of writers, newcomers and hugely experienced practitioners, and I've never met a writer in either camp who was not familiar with suffering.

Q. What has been one of your most rewarding experiences as a screenwriter and professor and why?

A. The most rewarding experience is seeing that early drafts that are lame and lackluster can, through diligence and effort and sweat, be made to shine. Again, discipline is the name of the game. One of my most successful students, superstar screenwriter David Koepp (*Jurassic Park, Mission Impossible, Spider-Man, War of the Worlds, Carlito's Way,* etc.) says that the secret of his career is his ability to slog through 17 drafts of a single script. It's vastly encouraging to see a writer who has yet to find the spark eventually find it and catch fire. Likewise, it's exciting to see from actual experience that hard work does indeed pay off. Interaction with students keeps screenwriting teachers fresh and alert and prevents us from falling into the ruts and grooves and grinds that can so readily afflict practitioners in a freelance enterprise such as screenwriting.

Sound Workers

OVERVIEW

Sound workers help create the audio aspects of a motion picture—from incidental music and sound effects, to the recording of dialogue and its final score.

HISTORY

You might be surprised to learn that early movies did not have sound as we know it today. Instead, dialogue and basic plot developments were written flashed on the screen as audiences watched movies. These silent movies were often accompanied by live musicians and orchestras, gramophone discs, sound effects workers, and live actors who provided dialogue, but they did not feature sound as we have become used to in modern motion pictures.

The world of filmmaking was changed forever with the emergence of sound technology systems that were created to be synchronized with the action taking place on screen. These early sound movies did not feature dialogue, but musical accompaniment. The first feature-length film that used this technology was *Don Juan* (1926). Other early sound features were *The Better 'Ole* (1926), *What Price Glory?* (1926), and *Sunrise* (1927).

During the late 1920s, movie studios spent millions of dollars to convert their facilities from silent to sound production. The studios also had to convert their movie theaters to sound presentation.

In 1927, *The Jazz Singer* became the first full-length movie to feature dialogue in addition to music. It was also the first full-length

In addition to creativity and musical ability, film composers must have strong computer skills in order to use software programs to help create their compositions. *(Chris Bergin, AP Photo/The Star Press)*

musical. *The Jazz Singer* was immensely popular and the motion picture industry quickly transitioned to sound. Filmsite.org reports that silent films had "practically disappeared" by 1930, and by 1940, "over 40 percent of the country's movie theatres had sound systems installed."

The Academy of Motion Picture Arts and Sciences recognized the importance of sound workers by creating several Academy Awards for sound professionals, including Sound Recording (1929–30), which was renamed to Sound Mixing in 2003; Music-Scoring (1934), which was renamed to Music-Original Score in 1999; Music-Song (1934), which was renamed to Music-Original Song in 1975; and Sound Effects (1963), which was renamed to Sound Editing in 2000.

Today, sound workers play a key role in lending authenticity and sheer entertainment value to movies.

THE JOB

The job title "sound worker" covers a wide variety of workers in the film industry who are responsible for creating sound for a film.

Top Film Scores

The following film scores (listed in alphabetical order) are widely considered to be among the best of the last four decades:

American Beauty, by Thomas Newman (1999)
Batman, by Danny Elfman (1989)
Close Encounters of the Third Kind, by John Williams (1977)
Dances with Wolves, by John Barry (1990)
Edward Scissorhands, by Danny Elfman (1990)
The Empire Strikes Back, by John Williams (1980)
E.T., by John Williams (1982)
Glory, by James Horner (1989)
Jaws, by John Williams (1975)
The Lord of the Rings: The Fellowship of the Ring, by Howard Shore (2001)
The Lord of the Rings: The Return of the King, by Howard Shore (2003)
The Mission, by Ennio Morricone (1986)
Out of Africa, by John Barry/Mozart (1985)
Poltergeist, by Jerry Goldsmith (1982)
Raiders of the Lost Ark, by John Williams (1981)
Schindler's List, by John Williams (1993)
Taxi Driver, by Bernard Herrmann (1975)

Sound workers are involved in all steps of the film production process. The following paragraphs detail some of the most popular career options for those interested in working with sound in the film industry. Most of these workers can find employment in other industries such as television, computer and video games, the performing arts, and other fields.

Composers write original scores and thematic music for films. A score is the music that plays throughout the film apart from any songs that may also be in the film. All composers use the same basic musical elements, including harmony, melody, counterpoint, and rhythm, but each composer applies these elements in a unique way. There is no prescribed way for a composer to go about composing. All composers work in a somewhat different way, but generally speaking they pursue their work in some kind of regular, patterned way, in much the same fashion of a novelist or a painter.

Songwriters write the words and music for songs that will appear in a film and/or on its soundtrack.

Arrangers take composers' musical compositions and transcribe them for other instruments or voices; work them into a score for a film; or adapt them to styles that are different from the one in which the music was written.

Music conductors direct large groups of musicians or singers in the performance of a piece of music that has been composed for a motion picture.

Musicians perform, compose, conduct, and arrange music for films.

Audio recording engineers and *sound engineering technicians* oversee the technical end of sound recording during filming or during the recording of a musical performance that will be used in a film.

Sound mixers, also known as *production sound mixers,* combine music and sound effects with a film's action. *Boom operators*, also known as *microphone boom operators,* work with sound mixers. They place and operate microphones to record dialogue and other sounds during filming. *Utility sound technicians* provide assistance to sound mixers and boom operators.

Recordists operate special audio recording equipment that is used during productions. *Playback operators* oversee audio equipment that is used to play back music for dancers and singers.

Sound designers oversee every aspect of the soundtrack of a movie. Some sound designers specialize in music and may have training in music theory or performance. Others work with sound effects. They may use unusual objects, machines, or computer-generated noisemakers to create a desired sound for a film. Sound designers often keep libraries of sounds that they reuse for various projects. These include natural sounds, such as thunder or raindrops, animal noises, motor sounds, or musical interludes.

Foley artists re-create and improve sound effects for a film during postproduction, matching the sounds with images.

Sound editors also work during the postproduction stage of a film. They edit recorded sound and dialogue to create the final soundtrack. They supervise Foley artists.

Music licensors negotiate with music labels and up-and-coming bands for the rights to use music in motion pictures. For larger films, a *music supervisor* may handle these licensing duties, as well as hire composers or songwriters to create music or songs for the film.

REQUIREMENTS

High School

All sound workers should learn as much as possible about music—especially as it relates to its use in motion pictures. Take as many music classes as possible and learn how to play one or more musical instruments, especially the piano, synthesizer, and keyboard. High school orchestras and bands are an excellent source for both practicing and studying music performance. The following paragraphs detail suggested classes and training for the various sound worker specialties.

There is no specific course of training that will help you to become a composer. Many composers begin composing from a very early age and receive tutoring and training to encourage their talent. Musically inclined students should continue their private studies and take advantage of everything musical their high school offers. If you are interested in creating music for motion pictures and television, you should listen to as many scores from these sources as possible. Specially gifted students usually find their way to schools or academies that specialize in music or the arts. These students may begin learning composition in this special environment, and some might begin to create original compositions.

If you are interested in becoming an audio recording engineer or technician, sound mixer, or other type of technical sound worker, you should take computer science, electronics (if offered), and math, including algebra and geometry.

Postsecondary Training

If you are interested in becoming a composer or musician, you can continue your education in any of numerous colleges and universities or special music schools or conservatories that offer bachelor's and higher degrees. Your course of study will include music history, music criticism, music theory, harmony, counterpoint, rhythm, melody, and ear training. In most major music schools, courses in composition are offered along with orchestration and arranging. Courses are also taught covering voice and the major musical instruments, including keyboard, guitar, and, more recently, synthesizer. Most schools now cover computer techniques as applied to music as well. Some schools offer concentrations or certificates in film and television scoring. Once such program is the Scoring for Motion Pictures and Television Program at the University of Southern California. Visit http://www.usc.edu/schools/music/programs/smptv for more information on this interesting program.

In the past, most sound designers learned their trade through on-the-job training. Today, many sound designers earn bachelor's degrees in music, sound design, or audio engineering, and this will probably become more necessary as technologies become more complex. Typical programs focus on computer and music studies, including music history, music theory, composition, sound design, and audio engineering.

Audio recording engineers, technicians, and mixers can prepare for the field by taking seminars and workshops and by pursuing degrees in music engineering and technology at technical schools or community colleges.

Other Requirements

All sound workers should have strong communication skills to be able to work with a diverse group of industry professionals and flexibility to work with a variety of musical genres. They should also be artistically talented, creative, and have good organizational skills.

EXPLORING

There are many ways to explore careers in motion picture sound. You can read books and magazines about audio and the movie industry, listen to film soundtracks of award-winning films, and read the biographies of well-known sound workers. One suggestion for those interested in becoming film music composers is *Inside Film Music: Composers Speak* (Los Angeles: Silman-James Press, 2007), by Christian Desjardins and Christopher Young. You can also visit music-related Web sites, including the following: *Film Music Magazine* (http://www.filmmusicmag.com), *Film Score Monthly* (http://www .filmscoremonthly.com), So You Want to be a Film Composer (from *Film Score Monthly*, http://www.filmscoremonthly.com/features/ beacomposer.asp), *695 Quarterly Magazine* (http://695quarterly .com), and Soundtrack.net (http://www.soundtrack.net). Finally, ask your music teacher or a school counselor to help arrange an information interview with a movie industry sound worker.

EMPLOYERS

Sound workers are employed by film production companies and any other organization that creates films. Many own their own businesses and offer their services to companies on a freelance basis.

STARTING OUT

Many sound professionals, especially composers and musicians, work on a freelance or project basis. Composers are self-employed. They complete their work in their own studios and then try to sell their pieces to music publishers, film and television production companies, or recording companies. Once their work becomes well known, clients, such as film and television producers, dance companies, or musical theater producers, may commission original pieces from composers. In this case, the client provides a story line, time period, mood, and other specifications the composer must honor in the creation of a musical score.

Some sound workers are lucky enough to learn the ins and outs of the field by working with well-know professionals in their field.

Sound workers should also consider joining music-related societies and associations such as the American Federation of Musicians; Meet the Composer; the American Composers Alliance; Broadcast Music, Inc.; the Society of Composers and Lyricists; American Society of Composers, Authors, and Publishers (ASCAP); Society of Professional Audio Recording Services; and Audio Engineering Society. These organizations provide job leads, professional support, and training opportunities.

ADVANCEMENT

Advancement for composers, arrangers, musicians, songwriters, and musical directors often takes place on a highly personal level. Composers, for example, may progress through their career to write or transcribe music of greater complexity and in more challenging structures. They may develop a unique style and even develop new forms and traditions of music. One day, their names might be added to the list of the great composers and arrangers. Some composers become well known for their work with film scores; John Williams, of *Star Wars* fame, is one.

Other types of sound workers advance by working on more prestigious films or working for larger companies. Some go on to write textbooks about their craft or teach at colleges and universities.

EARNINGS

Salaries for music directors, composers, arrangers, and orchestrators employed in all industries ranged from less than $21,480 to more than $85,020 in 2009, according to the U.S. Department of Labor (DOL). Median annual earnings for these workers were $45,090. Well-known composers and arrangers can earn salaries that exceed $150,000 a year.

Many composers, however, do not hold full-time salaried positions and are only paid in royalties for their compositions that sell. According to ASCAP, the royalty rate for 2007 was $.091 per song per album sold. The $.091 is divided between the composer and the publisher, based on their agreement. If the album sold 25,000 copies in 2007, the royalties the composer and publisher received would be $2,275. Naturally, if this song is the only one the composer has that brings in income during this time, his or her annual earnings are extremely low (keep in mind that the composer receives only a percentage of the $2,275).

On the other hand, a composer who creates music for a feature film may have substantial earnings, according to ASCAP. Factors that influence the composer's earnings include how much music is needed for the film, the film's total budget, if the film will be distributed to a general audience or have only limited showings, and the reputation of the composer. The ASCAP notes that depending on such factors, a composer can receive fees ranging from $20,000 for a lower-budget, small film to more than $1 million if the film is a big-budget release from a major studio and the composer is well known.

Musicians and singers employed in the motion picture and video industries earned mean hourly salaries of $34.98 in 2009—or $72,758 annually.

Sound engineering technicians employed in the motion picture and video industries earned mean annual salaries of $60,470 in 2009, according to the DOL.

The American Federation of Musicians of the United States and Canada has created pay scales for musicians and composers who perform or write music for motion picture and television films. Contact the federation for the latest rates.

Salaried sound workers receive typical fringe benefits such as paid vacation and sick days, health insurance, and the opportunity to participate in retirement savings plans. Freelance sound workers must pay for their own health insurance and other benefits. Freelance sound workers who belong to a union may receive some benefits as part of their membership package.

WORK ENVIRONMENT

Sound professionals work in a wide variety of settings. For example, composers and arrangers work in expensive, state-of-the-art home studios or in a bare room with an electric keyboard or a guitar depending on their preferences. Music conductors and musicians typically work in recording studios and concert halls. Sound designers, boom operators, mixers, and related workers work on film sets and on location throughout the world. Music licensors work in typical office settings. Sound workers often work under tight deadlines in order to meet production deadlines.

OUTLOOK

Overall employment in the motion picture and video industries is expected to grow faster than the average for all industries through 2018, according to the DOL. Competition for sound worker positions in the film industry is very strong. Sound workers with knowledge of filmmaking techniques will have better employment prospects than those with only a background in music or audio technology. Since it is very difficult to enter this career, many sound workers pursue related careers in other industries such as the performing arts, music and recording industry, and other fields.

FOR MORE INFORMATION

For profiles of composers of concert music, visit the ACA Web site.
American Composers Alliance (ACA)
802 West 190th Street, 1st Floor
New York, NY 10040-3937
Tel: 212-925-0458
E-mail: info@composers.com
http://www.composers.com

For educational resources, contact
American Composers Forum
332 Minnesota Street, Suite East 145
St. Paul, MN 55101-1300
Tel: 651-228-1407
http://www.composersforum.org

For career information, contact
American Federation of Musicians of the United States and Canada
1501 Broadway, Suite 600
New York, NY 10036-5505
Tel: 212-869-1330
http://www.afm.org

This union represents television and radio performers, including actors, announcers, dancers, disc jockeys, newspersons, singers, specialty acts, sportscasters, and stuntpersons.
American Federation of Television and Radio Artists
260 Madison Avenue
New York, NY 10016-2401
Tel: 212-532-0800
http://www.aftra.com

For articles on songwriting and practical information about the business of music, contact
American Society of Composers, Authors, and Publishers
One Lincoln Plaza
New York, NY 10023-7129
Tel: 212-621-6000
http://www.ascap.com

This organization "promotes the preservation of film and television music." Visit its Web site for more information.
The Film Music Society
1516 South Bundy Drive, Suite 305
Los Angeles, CA 90025-2683
Tel: 310-820-1909
E-mail: info@filmmusicsociety.org
http://www.filmmusicsociety.org

This branch of the alliance represents the interests of film and television sound and video workers.
International Alliance of Theatrical Stage Employees, Moving Picture Technicians, Artists and Allied Crafts of the United States, Its Territories, and Canada
Local 695
5439 Cahuenga Boulevard
North Hollywood, CA 91601-2918
Tel: 818-985-9204
http://www.695.com/html/toc.php

For information on sound editing, contact
Motion Picture Sound Editors
10061 Riverside Drive
PMB Box 751
Toluca Lake, CA 91602-2550
Tel: 818-506-7731

E-mail: mail@mpse.org
http://www.mpse.org

Visit the society's Web site for career resources, an online hall of fame, and information on The SCORE, *its quarterly publication.*
Society of Composers & Lyricists
8447 Wilshire Boulevard, Suite 401
Beverly Hills CA 90211-3209
Tel: 310-281-2812
http://www.thescl.com

Special and Visual Effects Technicians

OVERVIEW

Special and visual effects technicians are crafts persons who use technical skills to create effects, illusions, and computer-generated images for motion pictures, theater productions, television broadcasts and video games.

HISTORY

At the turn of the century a French magician-turned-filmmaker named Georges Melies invented motion picture special effects. To film futuristic space flight in *A Trip to the Moon,* he made a model of a rocket and fired it from a cannon in front of a painted backdrop. By the 1920s, special effects, or "tricks," had become a department of the major film studios, and technicians were steadily inventing new techniques and illusions. For a tornado scene in *The Wizard of Oz,* a miniature house was filmed falling from the studio ceiling, and when the film was reversed it became Dorothy's house flying into the air. Also in the *Wizard of Oz,* a 90-pound costume transformed actor Bert Lahr into the cowardly lion and extensive makeup and metalwork turned actor Jack Haley into the tin man. Effects departments still make extensive use of miniature models, which are easy to work with and save money.

In 1950 the Supreme Court broke up the movie studio monopolies. Independent, low-budget films began to proliferate and to affect audience tastes. They helped to make realistic, on-site shoots fashionable, and studio special effects departments became virtually extinct. It was not until the 1970s, when George Lucas brought his imagination and effects to *Star Wars,* that special effects were revived in force. Special effects, such as models and pyrotechnics, as well as early computer-generated imagery (visual effects) were used to create effects for the movie. The crew that Lucas assembled for that project formed the company Industrial Light & Magic (ILM), which remains a leader in a field that now includes hundreds of large and small special and visual effects companies. ILM has created special and visual effects for nearly 300 feature films, including 10 of the top 15 box office hits in movie history.

The industry toyed with computer-generated imagery (CGI) in the 1980s, with such films as *Tron* and *Star Trek II.* By the 1990s, the movie-going public was ready for an effects revolution, which began with James Cameron's *The Abyss* and *Terminator 2: Judgment Day* and reached full-force with 1993's *Jurassic Park. Twister* in 1996, *Titanic* in 1997, and *The Matrix* in 1999 raised the stakes for movie effects, and *Star Wars: Episode I-The Phantom Menace* used 2,000 digital shots (compared to *Titanic*'s 500). Today, visual effects technology is used extensively in the movie industry. In fact, the quality of computer-generated characters and scenery is so good in some movies (such as *Avatar*) that audiences have not been able to tell the difference between live action and computer-generated elements. *Avatar* won the Academy Award for Visual Effects in 2009.

Learn More About It

Debreceni, Todd. *Special Makeup Effects for Stage and Screen: Making and Applying Prosthetics.* St. Louis, Mo.: Focal Press, 2008.

Furniss, Maureen. *The Animation Bible: A Practical Guide to the Art of Animating from Flipbooks to Flash.* New York: Abrams, 2008.

Hahn, Don. *The Alchemy of Animation: Making an Animated Film in the Modern Age.* New York: Disney Editions, 2008.

Pinteau, Pascal. *Special Effects: An Oral History-Interviews with 37 Masters Spanning 100 Years.* New York: Harry N. Abrams, 2005.

Rickitt, Richard, and Ray Harryhausen. *Special Effects: The History and Technique.* 2d ed. New York: Billboard Books, 2007.

Slone, Michael. *Special Effects: How to Create a Hollywood Film Look on a Home Budget.* Studio City, Calif.: Michael Wiese Productions, 2007.

THE JOB

This article focuses on two types of effects technicians: special effects technicians and visual effects technicians. Both types create effects that amaze viewers as they watch movies, but they use different methods to go about creating movie magic. Special effects technicians deal with practical constructs and "in camera" effects—meaning those that are shot while the camera is rolling during a scene. Visual effects technicians use computer software programs to create scenes digitally or add or improve effects after a film is made. The following paragraphs provide more information on these two effects sectors.

Special Effects

Special effects technicians are crafts persons who build, install, and operate equipment used to produce the effects called for in scripts for motion picture, television, and theatrical productions. They read the script before filming to determine the type and number of special effects required. Depending on the effects needed for a production, they will mix chemicals, build large and elaborate sets or models, and fabricate costumes and other required backdrops from materials such as wood, metal, plaster, and clay.

What's known generally as special effects is actually a number of specialized trades. There are companies—known in the industry as special effects shops or houses—that offer specialized services in such diverse areas as computer animation, makeup, and mechanical effects. A special effects shop might provide just one or a combination of these services, and the crafts persons who work at the shops are often skilled in more than one area.

Makeup effects specialists create elaborate masks for actors to wear in a film or theatrical production. They also build prosthetic devices to simulate human—or nonhuman—limbs, hands, and heads. They work with a variety of materials, from latex plastic to create a monster's mask, to human hair they weave into wigs, to plain cotton cloth for a costume. They are skilled at sewing, weaving, applying makeup, and mixing colored dyes.

Mechanical effects specialists create effects such as rain, snow, and wind during movie productions. They may also build small sections of sets and backdrops that have an effect in them. They might also create moving or mechanized props, such as a futuristic automobile for a science fiction film. Because of a production's budget constraints, they are often required to construct miniature working models of such things as airplanes or submarines that, on film, will appear to be life- or larger-than-life-sized. Mechanical effects specialists are usually skilled in a number of trades, including plumbing, welding, carpentry, electricity, and robotics. At some film studios, the construction department may be responsible for some of the more labor-intensive responsibilities of mechanical effects specialists.

Pyrotechnic effects specialists are experts with munitions and firearms. They create carefully planned explosions for dramatic scenes in motion pictures and television broadcasts. They build charges and mix chemicals used for explosions according to strict legal standards.

Most professionals working in the field of special effects offer their services as freelance technicians. Some also work for special effects shops. The shops are contracted by motion picture or television broadcast producers and theatrical productions to provide the effects for a specific production. After reviewing the script and the type and number of the special effects required, the shop will send a special effects team to work on the production, or hire freelance technicians to assist on the job. Depending upon their level of expertise, many freelance technicians work for several shops.

Often, nonunion team members are required to help out with tasks that fall outside an area of expertise during the production. This may involve setting up and tearing down sets, moving heavy equipment, or pitching in on last-minute design changes. Union technicians are contracted to provide a specific service and rarely perform work outside an area of expertise.

Visual Effects

Computer animation specialists use high-tech computer programs to create entire movies (see the article Animators), scenes in movies, or effects that are otherwise impossible or too costly to build by traditional means. They typically work in an office, separate from the actual filming location. Because much of the technology they use is on the cutting edge of the industry, computer animation specialists are highly skilled in working with and developing unique computer applications and software programs.

Visual effects technicians often work as freelancers; some own their own businesses. Others may be employed as salaried workers by visual effects, animation, and film studios.

Special and visual effects coordinators lead teams of special effects or computer animation specialists to provide effects for motion pictures, television shows, and commercials.

REQUIREMENTS

High School

Special effects technicians rely on a mix of science and art. To prepare for this career, take all the art courses you can, including art history; many filmmakers look to classical art when composing shots and lighting effects. Photography courses will help you understand the use of light and shadow. Chemistry can give you some insight into the products you will be using. Working on high school drama productions can also be helpful for learning about lighting, makeup, and set and prop design.

Students who are interested in pursuing careers in visual effects should take computer science, animation, and other related classes.

Postsecondary Training

While there are no formal educational requirements for becoming a special or visual effects technician, some universities have film and television programs that include courses in special or visual effects. Some special effects technicians major in theater, art history, photography, and related subjects. Many colleges and universities offer master of fine arts degrees. These are studio programs in which you will be able to gain hands-on experience in theater production and filmmaking with a faculty composed of practicing artists.

Many of the skills required to work in mechanical effects can be gained by learning a trade such as carpentry, welding, plumbing, or hydraulics and applying those skills by building sets or props for community theater productions.

Some visual effects technicians working today have not had any special schooling or training, having mastered graphics programs on their own. Others have degrees in animation, computer science, software engineering, or related fields.

There are many schools that offer classes and degrees in animation. To find good schools offering animation and computer graphics programs, consult the Animation School Database of more than 900 schools around the world. The directory can be accessed for free at the Animation World Network's Web site, http://schools.awn.com.

Some special and visual effects technicians acquire their skills by participating in apprenticeships at movie and television studios.

Certification or Licensing

A mechanical special effects technician who works with fire and explosives generally needs a pyrotechnics operator's license issued by the state. A federal pyrotechnics license is also available.

Other Requirements

Special effects work is physically and mentally demanding. Technicians must be able to work as members of a team, following instructions carefully in order to avoid dangerous situations. They often work long days, so they must possess stamina. In addition, the work on a set can be uncomfortable; a mechanical effects specialist may have to work under adverse weather conditions or wait patiently in a small space for the cue to operate an effect. Makeup effects specialists spend most of their time working in a trailer on the set or in a shop where they construct and adjust the items required by the actors. Freelance technicians will often have to provide their own tools and equipment, which they either own or rent, when hired for a job.

Visual effects specialists should have patient personalities since they often work long hours at a computer, performing meticulous and sometimes repetitive work. Other important traits include the ability to work under deadline pressure, strong communication skills, and the ability to accept constructive criticism of their work.

Special and visual effects technicians must work both carefully and quickly; a mistake or a delay can become very expensive for the production company.

EXPLORING

Students who like to build things, who tend to be curious about how things work, or who enjoy working with computers, might be well suited to a career in special or visual effects. To learn more about the profession, visit your school or public library and bookstores to read more about the field. Browse magazine racks to find Hollywood trade magazines and other related material on your area of interest. *Animation Journal* (http://www.animationjournal.com), *Animation World* (http://www.awn.com/magazines/animation-world-magazine), *Cinefex* (http://www.cinefex.com), *Daily Variety* (http://www.variety.com), and *The Hollywood Reporter* (http://www.hollywoodreporter.com) are good places to start.

Since experience and jobs are difficult to get in the film and television industries, it is important to learn about the career to be sure it is right for you. Working on high school drama productions as a stagehand, "techie," or makeup artist can be helpful for learning set and prop design, methods of handling equipment, and artistry. Community theaters and independent filmmakers can provide volunteer work experience; they rely on volunteers because they have limited operating funds.

Alternatively, if you find you are adept in computer classes and curious about advances in computer animation, you may wish to pursue this field by continuing your learning and exploration of animation techniques.

EMPLOYERS

The top special and visual effects technicians work for special and visual effects houses. These companies contract with individual film productions; one film may have the effects created by more than one company. Major companies include Industrial Light & Magic (the *Star Wars* series, the *Harry Potter* series, *The Nightmare Before Christmas,* and *Avatar*). Other major companies include Digital Domain (*Titanic, Lord of the Rings: The Fellowship of the Ring,* and *Transformers*), and Rhythm & Hues Studios (*Aliens in the Attic, Night at the Museum,* and *The Chronicles of Narnia: The Lion, the Witch and the Wardrobe*). Some special and visual effects technicians own their own effects company or work on a freelance basis. Freelance technicians may work in several areas, doing theater work, film and television productions, and commercials.

STARTING OUT

Networking is an important aspect of finding work in the film industry. The Internet Movie Database (http://www.imdb.com) is an extensive listing of professionals in many aspects of the industry. Another good resource is LA411.com, an online directory of film industry professionals. Aspiring visual effects technicians can visit ttp://www.awn.com/magazines/vfx-world-magazine to obtain a list of potential employers.

Internships are another very good way to gain experience and make yourself a marketable job candidate. Film and theater companies are predominantly located in Los Angeles or New York, but there are opportunities elsewhere. Again, since theater and lower budget film productions operate with limited funds, you could find places to work for course credit or experience instead of a salary.

Special and visual effects shops are excellent places to try for an internship. You may find them in books and trade magazines, or try the yellow pages under theatrical equipment, theatrical makeup, theatrical and stage lighting equipment, or animation services. Even if one shop has no opportunities, it may be able to provide the name of another that takes interns.

You should keep a photographic record of all the work you do for theater and film productions, including photos of any drawings or sculptures you have done for art classes. It is important to have a portfolio or demo reel (a reel of film demonstrating your work) to send along with your resume to effects shops, makeup departments, and producers. If you want to work as a visual effects technician, you should create a demo CD or a Web site that features your work.

Special and visual effects technicians may choose to join a union; some film studios will only hire union members. Two of the major unions for special and visual effects technicians are the International Alliance of Theatrical Stage Employees, Moving Picture Technicians, Artists of the Allied Trades of the United States, Its Territories and Canada and Animators Guild Local 839.

ADVANCEMENT

Good special and visual effects technicians will acquire skills in several areas, becoming versatile and therefore desirable employees. Since many work on a freelance basis, it is useful to develop a good reputation and maintain contacts from past jobs. Successful technicians may be chosen to work on increasingly prestigious and challenging productions. Once they have a strong background and diverse experience, technicians may start their own shops.

EARNINGS

The salaries for special and visual effects technicians can vary widely. Motion picture projects may pay hundreds of dollars a week, but technicians may go months between projects.

The U.S. Department of Labor (DOL) does not provide information on salaries for special effects technicians. It does report that median weekly earnings of wage and salary workers in the motion picture and video industries were $627 in 2008.

Multimedia artists and animators who were employed in the motion picture and video industries earned annual mean salaries of $70,960 in 2009, according to the DOL. Salaries for all multimedia artists and animators ranged from less than $32,360 to more than $99,130. Technicians at some of the top effects houses can earn hundreds of thousands of dollars on a project.

Those working freelance will not have the benefits of full-time work, having to provide their own health insurance. Union members, however, often receive health insurance and other benefits of membership. Those working for special and visual effects houses receive the usual benefits including health insurance, bonuses, and retirement.

WORK ENVIRONMENT

Special and visual effects is an excellent field for someone who likes to dream up fantastic monsters and machines and has the patience to create them. Technicians must be willing to work long hours and have the stamina to work under strenuous conditions. Twelve-hour days are not uncommon, and to meet a deadline technicians may work for 15 hours a day. Many special and visual effects technicians work freelance, so there can be long periods of no work (and no pay) between jobs.

Because motion picture scripts often call for filming at various locations, special effects technicians may travel a great deal. Work environments can vary considerably; a technician may remain in a shop or at a computer terminal, or may go on location for a film or television shoot and work outdoors.

OUTLOOK

Competition for jobs in film special effects houses is fierce. There is heavy competition in this field, and in general the plum jobs go to the best trained. While some technicians provide special effects for theater, few find the work steady or well paying enough to work in theater exclusively. Most supplement their incomes by providing effects for television commercials and industrial productions as well.

Employment of animators (which includes visual effects technicians) who work in the motion picture and video industries is expected to grow much faster than the average for all careers through 2018, according to the DOL. Despite this prediction, competition for jobs is very strong since many people view this field as an exciting potential career path.

FOR MORE INFORMATION

For information about colleges with film and television programs of study, and to read interviews with filmmakers, visit the AFI Web site.
American Film Institute (AFI)
2021 North Western Avenue
Los Angeles, CA 90027-1657

Tel: 323-856-7600
http://www.afi.com

For information about animated films and digital effects, visit the AWN Web site, which includes feature articles, a list of schools, and a career section.
Animation World Network (AWN)
6525 Sunset Boulevard, Garden Suite 10
Hollywood, CA 90028-7212
Tel: 323-606-4200
E-mail: info@awn.com
http://www.awn.com

The guild represents the interests of animation professionals in California. Visit its Web site for information on training, earnings, and the animation industry.
Animators Guild Local 839
1105 North Hollywood Way
Burbank, CA 91505-2528
Tel: 818-845-7500
http://www.animationguild.org

For education and training information, check out the following Web site:
International Alliance of Theatrical Stage Employees, Moving
Picture Technicians, Artists and Allied Crafts of the United
States, Its Territories, and Canada
1430 Broadway, 20th Floor
New York, NY 10018-3348
Tel: 212-730-1770
http://www.iatse-intl.org

For membership and scholarship information, contact
International Animated Film Society-ASIFA Hollywood
2114 West Burbank Boulevard
Burbank, CA 91506-1232
Tel: 818-842-4691
E-mail: info@asifa-hollywood.org
http://www.asifa-hollywood.org

Visit the society's Web site for information about festivals and presentations and news about the industry.

Visual Effects Society
5535 Balboa Boulevard, Suite 205
Encino, CA 91316-1544
Tel: 818-981-7861
E-mail: info@visualeffectssociety.com
http://www.visualeffectssociety.com

This nonprofit organization represents the professional interests of women (and men) in animation. Visit its Web site for industry information, links to animation blogs, details on membership for high school students, and its quarterly newsletter.

Women in Animation
E-mail: wia@womeninanimation.org
http://wia.animationblogspot.com

Stunt Performers

OVERVIEW

Stunt performers, also called *stuntmen* and *stuntwomen,* are actors who perform dangerous scenes in motion pictures. They may fall off tall buildings, get knocked from horses and motorcycles, imitate fistfights, and drive in high-speed car chases. They must know how to set up stunts that are both safe to perform and believable to audiences. In these dangerous scenes, stunt performers are often asked to double, or take the place of, a star actor.

HISTORY

There have been stunt performers since the early years of motion pictures. Frank Hanaway, believed to be the first stunt performer, began his career in the 1903 film *The Great Train Robbery.* A former U.S. cavalryman, Hanaway had developed the skill of falling off a horse unharmed. Until the introduction of sound films in the 1920s, stunt performers were used mostly in slapstick comedy films, which relied on sight gags to entertain the audience.

The first stuntwoman in motion pictures was Helen Gibson, who began her stunt career in the 1914 film series *The Hazards of Helen.* Chosen for the job because of her experience performing tricks on horseback, Gibson went from doubling for Helen Holmes, the star actress, to eventually playing the lead role herself. Among her stunts was jumping from a fast-moving motorcycle onto an adjacent moving locomotive.

Despite the success of Helen Gibson, most stunt performers were men. For dangerous scenes, actresses were usually doubled by a stuntman wearing a wig and the character's costume. Because films usually showed stunts at a distance, audiences could not tell the switch had been made.

Discrimination in the film industry also resulted in few minorities working as stunt performers. White men doubled for American Indians, Asians, Mexicans, and African Americans by applying makeup or other material to their skin. This practice was called "painting down."

As the motion picture industry grew, so did the importance of stunt performers. Because injury to a star actor could end a film project and incur a considerable financial loss for the studio, producers would allow only stunt performers to handle dangerous scenes. Even so, star actors would commonly brag that they had performed their own stunts. Only a few, such as Helen Gibson and Richard Talmadge, actually did.

Beginning in the 1950s the growth in the number of independent, or self-employed, producers brought new opportunities for stunt performers. In general, independent producers were not familiar with stunt work and came to rely on experienced stunt performers to set up stunt scenes and to find qualified individuals to perform them. Stunt performers who did this kind of organizational work came to be called *stunt coordinators*.

The Stuntmen's Association, the first professional organization in the field, was founded in 1960. Its goal was to share knowledge of stunt techniques and safety practices, to work out special problems concerning stunt performers, and to help producers find qualified stunt performers. Other organizations followed, including the International Stunt Association, the Stuntwomen's Association, the United Stuntwomen's Association, Stunts Unlimited, and Drivers Inc. As a result of these organizations, stunt performers are now better educated and trained in stunt techniques.

An increasing number of women and minorities have become stunt performers since the 1970s. The Screen Actors Guild (SAG), the union that represents stunt performers, has been at the vanguard of this change. In the 1970s SAG banned the practice of painting down, thus forcing producers to find, for example, an African-American stuntman to double for an African-American actor. SAG also began to require that producers make an effort to find female stunt performers to double for actresses. Only after showing that a number of qualified stuntwomen have declined the role can a producer hire a stuntman to do the job.

Over the years, new technology has changed the field of stunt work. Air bags, for example, make stunts safer, and faster cars and better brakes have given stunt performers more control. Stunt performers, however, still rely on their athletic ability and sense of timing when doing a dangerous stunt.

A student practices falls during a class session at the International Stunt School in Seattle, Washington. *(Ted S. Warren, AP Photo)*

THE JOB

Stunt performers work on a wide variety of scenes that have the potential for causing serious injury, including car crashes and chases; fist and sword fights; falls from cars, motorcycles, horses, and buildings; airplane and helicopter gags; rides through river rapids;

Learn More About It

Bill, Tony. *Movie Speak: How to Talk Like You Belong on a Movie Set*. New York: Workman Publishing Company, 2009.
Boughn, Jenn. *Stage Combat: Fisticuffs, Stunts, and Swordplay for Theater and Film*. New York: Allworth Press, 2006.
Walter, Mike S. *Hollywood Stuntman Comes Clean: What Hurts the Most?* Bloomington, Ind.: iUniverse Inc., 2007.
Wolf, Steve. *The Secret Science Behind Movie Stunts & Special Effects*. Costa Mesa, Calif.: Saddleback Educational Publishing, 2008.

and confrontations with animals, such as in a buffalo stampede. Although they are hired as actors, they only occasionally perform a speaking role. Some stunt performers specialize in one type of stunt.

There are two general types of stunt roles: double and nondescript. The first requires a stunt performer to "double"—to take the place of—a star actor in a dangerous scene. As a double, the stunt performer must portray the character in the same way as the star actor. A nondescript role does not involve replacing another person and is usually an incidental character in a dangerous scene. An example of a nondescript role is a driver in a freeway chase scene.

The idea for a stunt usually begins with the screenwriter. Stunts can make a movie not only exciting, but also profitable. Action films, in fact, make up the majority of box-office hits. The stunts, however, must make sense within the context of the film's story.

Once the stunts are written into the script, it is the job of the director to decide how they will appear on the screen. Directors, especially of large, action-filled movies, often seek the help of a stunt coordinator. Stunt coordinators are individuals who have years of experience performing or coordinating stunts and who know the stunt performer community well. A stunt coordinator can quickly determine if a stunt is feasible and, if so, what is the best and safest way to perform it. The stunt coordinator plans the stunt, oversees the setup and construction of special sets and materials, and either hires or recommends the most qualified stunt performer. Some stunt coordinators also take over the direction of action scenes. Because of this responsibility, many stunt coordinators are members of both the Screen Actors Guild and the Directors Guild of America.

Although a stunt may last only a few seconds on film, preparations for the stunt can take several hours or even days. Stunt performers work with such departments as props, makeup, wardrobe, and set design. They also work closely with the special effects team to resolve technical problems and ensure safety. The director and the stunt performer must agree on a camera angle that will maximize the effect of the stunt. These preparations can save a considerable amount of production time and money. A carefully planned stunt can often be completed in just one take. More typically, the stunt person will have to perform the stunt several times until the director is satisfied with the performance.

Stunt performers do not have a death wish. They are dedicated professionals who take great precautions to ensure their safety. Air bags, body pads, or cables might be used in a stunt involving a fall or a crash. If a stunt performer must enter a burning building, special fireproof clothing is worn and protective cream is applied to the skin. Stunt performers commonly design and build their own protective equipment.

Stunt performers are not only actors but also athletes. Thus, they spend much of their time keeping their bodies in top physical shape and practicing their stunts.

REQUIREMENTS

High School

Take physical education, dance, and other courses that will involve you in exercise, weight lifting, and coordination. Sports teams can help you develop the athletic skills needed. In a theater class, you will learn to take direction, and you may have the opportunity to perform for an audience.

Postsecondary Training

There is no minimum educational requirement for becoming a stunt performer. Most learn their skills by working for years under an experienced stunt performer. A number of stunt schools, however, do exist, including the United Stuntmen's Association International Stunt School. You can also benefit from enrolling in theater classes.

Among the skills that must be learned are specific stunt techniques, such as how to throw a punch; the design and building of safety equipment; and production techniques, such as camera angles and film editing. The more a stunt performer knows about all aspects of filmmaking, the better that person can design effective and safe stunts.

Certification or Licensing

There is no certification available, but, like all actors, stunt performers working in film and TV must belong to the Screen Actors Guild (SAG). Many stunt performers also belong to the American Federation of Television and Radio Artists (AFTRA). As a member of a union, you'll receive special benefits, such as better pay and compensation for overtime and holidays.

Other Requirements

Stunt work requires excellent athletic ability. Many stunt performers were high school and college athletes, and some were Olympic or world champions. Qualities developed through sports such as self-discipline, coordination, common sense, and coolness under stress are essential to becoming a successful stunt performer. As a stunt performer, you must exercise regularly to stay in shape and maintain good health. And since you may be working with ropes, cables, and other equipment, you should also have some understanding of the mechanics of the stunts you will be performing.

Because much of the work involves being a stunt double for a star actor, it is helpful to have a common body type. Exceptionally tall or short people, for example, may have difficulty finding roles.

EXPLORING

There are few means of gaining experience as a stunt performer prior to actual employment. Involvement in high school or college athletics is helpful, as is acting experience in a school or local theater. As an intern or extra for a film production, you may have the opportunity to see stunt people at work. Theme parks and circuses also make much use of stunt performers; some of these places allow visitors to meet the performers after shows.

EMPLOYERS

Most stunt performers work on a freelance basis, contracting with individual productions on a project-by-project basis. Stunt performers working on TV projects may have long-term commitments if serving as a stand-in for a regular character. Some stunt performers also work in other aspects of the entertainment industry, taking jobs with theme parks, and live stage shows and events.

STARTING OUT

Most stunt performers enter the field by contacting stunt coordinators and asking for work. Coordinators and stunt associations can be located in trade publications. To be of interest to coordinators, you'll need to promote any special skills you have, such as stunt driving, skiing, and diving. Many stunt performers also have agents who locate work for them, but an agent can be very difficult to get if you have no stunt experience. If you live in New York or Los Angeles, you should volunteer to work as an intern for an action film; you may have the chance to meet some of the stunt performers, and make connections with crew members and other industry professionals. You can also submit a resume to the various online services that are used by coordinators and casting directors. If you attend a stunt school, you may develop important contacts in the field.

ADVANCEMENT

New stunt performers generally start with simple roles, such as being one of 40 people in a fight scene. With greater experience and training, stunt performers can get more complicated roles. Some stunt associations have facilities where stunt performers work out and practice their skills. After a great deal of experience, you may be invited to join a professional association such as the Stuntmen's Association of Motion Pictures, which will allow you to network with others in the industry.

About five to 10 years of experience are usually necessary to become a stunt coordinator. Some stunt coordinators eventually work as a director of action scenes. These professionals are known as *second unit directors*.

EARNINGS

The earnings of stunt performers vary considerably by their experience and the difficulty of the stunts they perform. In 2010, the minimum daily salary of stunt performers and coordinators in the motion picture and television industries was $809. Stunt performers and coordinators working on a weekly basis in either motion pictures or television earned a minimum of $3,015 per week. Though this may seem like a lot of money, few stunt performers work every day. According to the SAG, the majority of its members make less than $7,500. But those who are in high demand can receive salaries of well over $100,000 a year.

Stunt performers usually negotiate their salaries with the stunt coordinator. In general, they are paid per stunt; if they have to repeat the stunt three times before the director likes the scene, the stunt performer gets paid three times. If footage of a stunt is used in another film, the performer is paid again. The more elaborate and dangerous the stunt, the more money the stunt performer receives. Stunt performers are also compensated for overtime and travel expenses. Stunt coordinators negotiate their salaries with the producer.

WORK ENVIRONMENT

The working conditions of a stunt performer change from project to project. It could be a studio set, a river, or an airplane thousands of feet above the ground. Like all actors, they are given their own dressing rooms.

Careers in stunt work tend to be short. The small number of jobs is one reason, as are age and injury. Even with the emphasis on safety, injuries commonly occur, often because of mechanical failure, problems with animals, or human error. The possibility of death is always present. Despite these drawbacks, a large number of people are attracted to the work because of the thrill, the competitive challenge, and the chance to work in motion pictures.

OUTLOOK

There are more than 7,700 stunt performers who belong to the SAG, but only a fraction of those can afford to devote themselves to film work full time. Stunt coordinators will continue to hire only very experienced professionals, making it difficult to break into the business.

The future of the profession may be affected by computer technology. In more cases, filmmakers may choose to use special effects and computer-generated imagery for action sequences. Not only can computer effects allow for more ambitious images, but they are also safer. Safety on film sets has always been a serious concern; despite innovations in filming techniques, stunts remain very dangerous. However, using live stunt performers can give a scene more authenticity, so talented stunt performers will always be in demand.

FOR MORE INFORMATION

This union represents film and television performers. It has general information on actors, directors, and producers.

Screen Actors Guild
5757 Wilshire Boulevard, 7th Floor
Los Angeles, CA 90036-3600
Tel: 323-954-1600
http://www.sag.org

For information on opportunities in the industry, contact the following organizations:

Stuntmen's Association of Motion Pictures
5200 Lankersheim Boulevard, Suite 190
North Hollywood, CA 91601-3100
Tel: 818-766-4334
E-mail: hq@stuntmen.com
http://www.stuntmen.com

Stuntwomen's Association of Motion Pictures
Tel: 818-762-0907
E-mail: stuntwomen@stuntwomen.com
http://www.stuntwomen.com

Talent Agents and Scouts

QUICK FACTS

School Subjects
Business
Theater/dance

Personal Skills
Communication/ideas
Leadership/management

Work Environment
Primarily indoors
Primarily one location

Minimum Education Level
Bachelor's degree

Salary Range
$25,860 to $119,550 to
$150,000+

Certification or Licensing
Required by certain states

Outlook
Much faster than the average

DOT
191

GOE
01.01.01

NOC
5124

O*NET-SOC
13–1011.00

OVERVIEW

An *agent* is a salesperson who sells artistic or athletic talent. *Talent agents* act as representatives for actors, directors, writers, models, athletes, and other people who work in the arts, advertising, sports, and fashion. (This article focuses primarily on agents in film.) Agents promote their clients' talent and manage their legal contractual business.

HISTORY

The wide variety of careers that exists in the film and television industries today evolved gradually. In the 19th century in England and America, leading actors and actresses developed a system, called the "actor-manager system," in which the actor both performed and handled business and financial arrangements. Over the course of the 20th century, responsibilities diversified. In the first decades of the century, major studios took charge of the actors' professional and financial management.

In the 1950s the major studio monopolies were broken, and control of actors and contracts came up for grabs. Resourceful business-minded people became agents when they realized that there was money to be made by controlling access to the talent behind movie and television productions. They became middlemen between actors (and other creative people) and the production studios, charging commissions for use of their clients.

Currently, commissions range between 10 and 15 percent of the money an actor earns in a production. In more recent years, agents have formed revolutionary deals for their stars, making more money for agencies and actors alike. Powerful agencies such as Creative Artists Agency, International Creative Management, and the William Morris Agency are credited with (or, by some, accused of) heralding in the age of the multimillion-dollar deal for film stars. This has proved controversial, as some top actor fees have inflated to more than $20 million per picture; some industry professionals worry that high actor salaries are cutting too deeply into film budgets, while others believe that actors are finally getting their fair share of the profits. Whichever the case, the film industry still thrives, and filmmakers still compete for the highest priced talent. And the agent, always an active player in the industry, has become even more influential in how films are made.

THE JOB

Talent agents act as representatives for actors, writers, and others who work in the entertainment industry. They look for clients who have potential for success and then work aggressively to promote their clients to film and television directors, casting directors, production companies, advertising companies, and other potential employers. Agents work closely with clients to find assignments that will best achieve clients' career goals.

Some agents also work as *talent scouts*. These workers actively search for new clients, whom they then bring to an agency. Or the clients themselves might approach agents who have good reputations and request their representation.

Agents and scouts find clients in several ways. Those who work for an agency might be assigned a client by the agency, based on experience or a compatible personality. Some agents also work as talent scouts and actively search for new clients, whom they then bring to an agency. Or the clients themselves might approach agents who have good reputations and request their representation. Agents involved in the film and television industries review portfolios, screen tests, and audiotapes to evaluate potential clients' appearance, voice, personality, experience, ability to take direction, and other factors.

When an agent agrees to represent a client, they both sign a contract that specifies the extent of representation, the time period, payment, and other legal considerations.

When agents look for jobs for their clients, they do not necessarily try to find as many assignments as possible. Agents try to carefully choose assignments that will further their clients' careers. For example, an agent might represent an actor who wants to work in film, but is having difficulty finding a role. The agent looks for roles in commercials, music videos, or voice-overs that will give the actor some exposure.

Agents also work closely with the potential employers of their clients. They need to satisfy the requirements of both parties. Agents who represent actors have a network of directors, producers, advertising executives, and photographers that they contact frequently to see if any of their clients can meet their needs.

When agents see a possible match between employer and client, they speak to both and quickly organize meetings, interviews, or auditions so that employers can meet potential hires and evaluate their work and capabilities. Agents must be persistent and aggressive on behalf of their clients. They spend time on the phone with employers, convincing them of their clients' talents and persuading them to hire clients. There may be one or several interviews, and the agent may coach clients through this process to make sure clients understand what the employer is looking for and adapt their presentations accordingly. When a client achieves success and is in great demand, the agent receives calls, scripts, and other types of work requests and passes along only those that are appropriate to the interests and goals of the client.

When an employer agrees to hire a client, the agent helps negotiate a contract that outlines salary, benefits, promotional appearances, and other fees, rights, and obligations. Agents have to look out for the best interests of their clients and at the same time satisfy employers in order to establish continuing, long-lasting relationships.

In addition to promoting individuals, agents may also work to make package deals—for example, combining a writer, director, and a star to make up a package, which they then market to production studios. The agent charges a packaging commission to the studio in addition to the commissions agreed to in each package member's contract. A strong package can be very lucrative for the agency or agencies that represent the talent involved, since the package commission is often a percentage of the total budget of the production.

Agents often develop lifelong working relationships with their clients. They act as business associates, advisers, advocates, mentors, teachers, guardians, and confidantes. Because of the complicated nature of these relationships, they can be volatile, so a successful relationship requires trust and respect on both sides, which can only be earned through experience and time. Agents who represent high-profile talent make up only a small percentage of agency work. Most agents represent lesser-known or locally known talent.

The largest agencies are located in Los Angeles and New York, where film, theater, advertising, publishing, fashion, and art-buying industries are centered. There are modeling and theatrical agencies in most large cities, however, and independent agents are established throughout the country.

REQUIREMENTS

High School
You should take courses in business, mathematics, and accounting to prepare for the management aspects of an agent's job. Take English and speech courses to develop good communication skills because an agent must be gifted at negotiation. You also need a good eye for talent, so you need to develop some expertise in film, theater, art, literature, advertising, sports, or whatever field you hope to specialize in.

Postsecondary Training
There are no formal requirements for becoming an agent, but a bachelor's degree is strongly recommended. Advanced degrees in law and business are becoming increasingly prevalent; law and business training are useful because agents are responsible for writing contracts according to legal regulations. However, in some cases an agent may obtain this training on the job. Agents come from a variety of backgrounds; some of them have worked as actors and then shifted into agent careers because they enjoyed working in the industry. Agents who have degrees from law or business schools have an advantage when it comes to advancing their careers or opening a new agency.

Certification or Licensing
Licensing requirements vary by state. Contact your state's department of professional regulation for information about requirements in your state. Agents can become franchised by the Screen Actors Guild (SAG). (According to SAG, the franchise designation "reflects only that the agent or agency is state licensed where required; has provided a surety bond or other security; has submitted recommendations from people in the industry; and has promised to comply with SAG rules governing agents and agencies.")

Other Requirements
It is most important to be willing to work hard and aggressively pursue opportunities for clients. You should be detail oriented and have a good head for business; contract work requires meticulous attention to detail. You need a great deal of self-motivation and

ambition to develop good contacts in industries that may be difficult to break into. You should be comfortable talking with all kinds of people and be able to develop relationships easily. It helps to be a good general conversationalist in addition to being knowledgeable about your field.

EXPLORING

To learn more about working as an agent in the film and television industries, read publications agents read, such as *Variety* (http://www.variety.com), *The Hollywood Reporter* (http://www .hollywoodreporter.com), and *Entertainment Weekly* (http://www .ew.com/ew). See current movies to get a sense of the established and up-and-coming talents in the film industry. Trace the careers of actors you like, including their early work in independent films, commercials, and stage work.

If you live in Los Angeles or New York, you may be able to volunteer or intern at an agency to find out more about the career. If you live outside Los Angeles and New York, search the Web for listings of local agencies. Most major cities have agents who represent local performing artists, actors, and models. If you contact them, they may be willing to offer you some insight into the nature of talent management in general.

EMPLOYERS

Talent agencies are located all across the United States, handling a variety of talents. Those agencies that represent artists and professionals in the film industry are located primarily in Los Angeles. Some film agencies, such as the William Morris Agency, have offices in New York. An agency may specialize in a particular type of talent, such as minority actors, extras, or TV commercial actors.

STARTING OUT

The best way to enter this field is to seek an internship with an agency. If you live in or can spend a summer in Los Angeles or New York, you have an advantage in terms of numbers of opportunities. Libraries and bookstores will have resources for locating talent agencies. By searching the Web, you can find many free listings of reputable agents. The Screen Actors Guild also maintains a list of franchised agents that is available on its Web site. The Yellow Pages will yield a list of local talent agencies. For those who live in

Los Angeles, there are employment agencies that deal specifically with talent agent careers. Compile a list of agencies that may offer internship opportunities. Some internships will be paid and others may provide college course credit, but most importantly, they will provide you with experience and contacts in the industry. An intern who works hard and knows something about the business stands a good chance of securing an entry-level position at an agency. At the top agencies, this will be a position in the mailroom, where almost everyone starts. In smaller agencies, it may be an assistant position. Eventually persistence, hard work, and cultivated connections will lead to a job as an agent.

ADVANCEMENT

Once you have a job as an assistant, you will be allowed to work closely with an agent to learn the ropes. You may be able to read contracts and listen in on phone calls and meetings. You will begin to take on some of your own clients as you gain experience. Agents who wish to advance must work aggressively on behalf of their clients as well as seek out quality talent to bring into an agency. Those who are successful command more lucrative salaries and may choose to open their own agencies. Some agents find that their work is a good stepping-stone toward a different career in the industry.

EARNINGS

Earnings for agents vary greatly, depending on the success of the agent and his or her clients. An agency receives 10 to 15 percent of a client's fee for a project. An agent is then paid a commission by the agency as well as a base salary. Talent agents in the movie industry earned mean annual salaries of $119,550 in 2009, according to the U.S. Department of Labor. Salaries for agents and business managers employed in all industries ranged from less than $25,860 to more than $150,000 annually.

Working for an agency, an experienced agent will receive health and retirement benefits, bonuses, and paid travel and accommodations.

WORK ENVIRONMENT

Work in a talent agency can be lively and exciting. It is rewarding to watch a client attain success with your help. The work can seem very glamorous, allowing you to rub elbows with the rich and famous and make contacts with the most powerful people in the entertainment industry. Most agents, however, represent less famous actors, directors, and other industry professionals.

Agents' work requires a great deal of stamina and determination in the face of setbacks. The work can be extremely stressful, even in small agencies. It often demands long hours, including evenings and weekends. To stay successful, agents at the top of the industry must constantly network. They spend a great deal of time on the telephone, with both clients and others in the industry, and attending industry functions.

OUTLOOK

Employment in the arts and entertainment field is expected to grow rapidly in response to the demand for entertainment from a growing population. However, the numbers of artists and performers also continues to grow, creating fierce competition for all jobs in this industry. This competition will drive the need for more agents and scouts to find talented individuals and place them in the best jobs.

Despite a plethora of entertainment options available today, the American public retains a strong love of movies—whether viewed in theaters, at home, or on mobile devices. With markets overseas expanding, even the films that don't do so well domestically can still turn a tidy profit. As a result, agents at all levels in the film industry will continue to thrive. Also, more original cable television programming will lead to more actors and performers seeking representation.

FOR MORE INFORMATION

For industry news, contact
Association of Talent Agents
9255 Sunset Boulevard, Suite 930
Los Angeles, CA 90069-3317
Tel: 310-274-0628
http://www.agentassociation.com

For general information on management careers in the performing arts, contact
North American Performing Arts Managers and Agents
459 Columbus Avenue, Suite 133
New York, NY 10024-5129
E-mail: conal@napama.org
http://www.napama.org

Visit the SAG Web site for information about acting in films and for a list of talent agencies.

Screen Actors Guild (SAG)
5757 Wilshire Boulevard, 7th Floor
Los Angeles, CA 90036-3600
Tel: 323-954-1600
http://www.sag.org

Index

Entries and page numbers in **bold** indicate major treatment of a topic.